ASSESSING THE U.S.-QATAR RELATIONSHIP

HEARING

BEFORE THE

SUBCOMMITTEE ON
THE MIDDLE EAST AND NORTH AFRICA

OF THE

COMMITTEE ON FOREIGN AFFAIRS
HOUSE OF REPRESENTATIVES

ONE HUNDRED FIFTEENTH CONGRESS

FIRST SESSION

JULY 26, 2017

Serial No. 115–55

Printed for the use of the Committee on Foreign Affairs

Available via the World Wide Web: http://www.foreignaffairs.house.gov/ or
http://www.gpo.gov/fdsys/

U.S. GOVERNMENT PUBLISHING OFFICE

26–427PDF   WASHINGTON : 2017

CONTENTS

ASSESSING THE U.S.-QATAR RELATIONSHIP

WEDNESDAY, JULY 26, 2017

House of Representatives,
Subcommittee on the Middle East and North Africa,
Committee on Foreign Affairs,
Washington, DC.

The subcommittee met, pursuant to notice, at 2:16 p.m., in room 2172, Rayburn House Office Building, Hon. Ileana Ros-Lehtinen (chairman of the subcommittee) presiding.

Ms. Ros-Lehtinen. The subcommittee will come to order. After recognizing myself and Ranking Member Deutch for 5 minutes each for our opening statements, I will then recognize other members seeking recognition for 1 minute. We will then hear from our witnesses.

And without objection, witnesses, your prepared statements will be made a part of the record, and members may have 5 days to insert statements and questions for the record, subject to the length limitation in the rules.

We have many members of our subcommittee who are also on the Judiciary Committee, including Ranking Member Deutch, and there is an important markup happening as we speak. So you might see a lot of members moving back and forth, and we appreciate the time they can spare to come over here.

Thank you, Mr. Deutch.

The Chair now recognizes herself for 5 minutes.

Last month, this subcommittee convened a hearing on the challenges and opportunities for the United States Saudi Arabia bilateral relationship. Today, we focus on the U.S.-Qatar relationship and Qatar's relationship with its neighbors.

I think it is important to note that this rift in the Gulf is not new. Katherine Bauer, a former senior-level official at the Treasury Department stated earlier this month at a think tank event, "Saudi Arabia and the UAE have sought for years to kind of galvanize Qatar's actions against the terrorist financiers that were operating and continue to operate in Qatar."

Qatar has been known to be a permissive environment for terror financing, reportedly funding U.S. designated foreign terrorist organizations, such as Hamas, as well as several extremist groups operating in Syria.

In 2014, the former deputy director of CIA, David Cohen, called out Qatar publicly along with the Kuwaitis, because according to him, "The private engagement with these countries had not achieved what we were trying to achieve."

In fact, Qatar has openly housed Hamas leaders, Taliban leaders, and has several individuals who have been sanctioned by our U.S. Treasury Department, and it has failed to prosecute them.

At least one high-ranking Qatari official provided support to the mastermind of the 9/11 terror attacks against our country, Khalid Sheikh Mohammad. Then, of course, there is Khalifa Mohammed, who is a U.S.-, EU-, and U.N.-designated international terrorist for his role in financing al-Qaeda and the 9/11 mastermind.

In 2008, he was tried and convicted in absentia by Bahrain for his terrorist activity, and arrested later that year by Qatar only to be released by the Qataris 6 months later, and then openly financed by Doha.

Can anyone guess what Khalifa Mohammed has been up to these days? He was implicated in terror financing activities in 2012, but more recently, he has been alleged to be financing and supporting terror in both Iraq and Syria with no response from the Qatari Government.

Hamas leader, Khaled Meshaal, also made Doha his headquarters for years while the Qatari's—with the Qatari's Government support and even the Muslim Brotherhood has received significant support from Qatar.

Of course, not all of this is supported by the government in Doha. Many individuals and charities in Qatar have been known to raise large sums of money for al-Qaeda, the Nusra front, Hamas, and even ISIS. In Qatar, there are three buckets: Terror financing by the government; terror financing done in Qatar through their own citizens that their government may not know about; and terror financing in Qatar that the government knows about but does nothing to stop.

According to the 2015 country reports on terrorism, the State Department stated, "Entities and individuals within Qatar continue to serve as a source of financial support for terrorists and violent extremist groups, particularly regional al-Qaeda affiliates such as the Nusra front."

There is no excuse for openly harboring terrorist and supporting groups that seek to harm our allies, and the excuse by Qatar that it is harboring these nefarious actors is because the U.S. asked them to no longer stands up.

Qatar should not be continuing this reckless policy due to past mistakes from previous Republican and Democratic administrations. We must not allow for our air base to be used as a means to justify this sort of behavior, and a lack of a more appropriate response.

Doha's behavior must change the status quo, and if it does not, it risks losing our cooperation on the air base. The truth of the matter is that none of the Gulf countries—none of the Gulf countries are without their issues. All of the nations have been involved in funding different groups at some point that we would not approve of. But it seems like Saudi Arabia and the UAE are making progress at a faster rate while Qatar is making some progress but still is lagging slowly behind.

According to the Congressional Research Service, "In October 2016, Daniel Glaser, then Assistant Secretary for Terrorist Financing in the Office for Terrorism and Financial Intelligence, told the

Washington, DC, Research Institute that over the past decade, Qatar has made less progress in countering terrorism financing than had Saudi Arabia."

We must analyze the totality of our relationship with these Gulf countries. While Qatar only helps to facilitate our operations at our air base, the UAE, for example, has spent 12 years with us fighting alongside in Afghanistan and has been involved in counterterrorism operations with the U.S. in Libya.

So moving forward, one outcome that I hope comes out of this dispute is for the Gulf countries to work closely with our Treasury Department's Financial Action Task Force to root out and disrupt terror financing streams. This uneasy time may just be an opportunity for us to take a long hard look at how, and for some, if, we can effectively address and stop terror financing in the region, and ultimately defeat the extremism that threatens the security of us all.

And with that, I turn to my friend, the ranking member, Mr. Deutch, for his statement.

Mr. DEUTCH. Thank you, Madam Chairwoman.

Thanks to the witnesses for being back before our committee. I thank the chairman for convening today's timely hearing to explore our relationship with Qatar at a moment of great instability in the region.

The ongoing diplomatic rift between Qatar and its Gulf neighbors is not good for the parties of the conflict; it is not good for the region; and it is not good for American interests. It is a distraction from today's most pressing challenges, Iran's destabilizing activities, the conflict in Syria, and the spread of terrorism.

For most Americans who expect conflict in the Middle East to fall along sectarian lines, or between competing regional hegemons, it is confusing to see Sunni Arab neighbors in conflict. But this is a dispute over longstanding grievances, over Qatar's support financially, and through its state-owned Al Jazeera news station, for actors and groups that Qatar's neighbors and, in many cases, the United States, see as deeply problematic.

This feud, like others in the region, is a nuanced and deeply complex matter, and our relationship with Qatar is no less complex.

A tiny but immensely wealthy nation pursues an ambitious foreign policy of close relations with all actors in the region. Unfortunately, this includes terror groups like Hamas and the Afghan Taliban. Qatar has served as a financial and political lifeline for Hamas' devastating rule in Gaza since the terror group took over more than a decade ago.

Qatar has sent hundreds of millions of dollars into the Gaza strip, provides safe haven in Doha for Hamas leader, Khaled Meshaal, and helped legitimize Hamas rule in 2012 when the Emir became the first international leader to visit Hamas-led territory.

Qatar has also supported other dangerous groups in the region, including sending advanced weaponry and financing to extremist elements in Syria and Libya, and Al Jazeera has given voice to clerics calling for suicide attacks against Americans and Israelis.

These realities are troubling. But Qatar is also a close partner in our fight against terrorism in the region. Doha hosts and helps fund the largest U.S. military facility in the Middle East, essentially our forward operating base for U.S. Central Command. It is from this base that we supported the wars in Iraq and Afghanistan, and are, today, flying air strikes against ISIS.

Qatar has also helped to serve as regional mediator oftentimes to the benefit of the United States. Qatar has helped broker ceasefires between Hamas and Israel during periods of intense fighting. The Qataris also helped secure the release of Peter Theo Curtis, an American hostage held for nearly 2 years by the al-Qaeda linked Nusra front in Syria just days after that tragic beheading of fellow American journalist, James Foley.

Qatar has also provided the U.S. with valuable and actionable intelligence on the financing streams for ISIS and has begun taking steps to hold Qatar accountable for terror financing. But they have got a lot more to do.

While they have begun prosecuting Qataris for sending money to terror groups, they have done so in secret, hardly an effective deterrent, and it is unclear whether the outcomes of these prosecutions have led to any significant jail time or penalty.

I was pleased to see the signing of a new memorandum of understanding with Secretary Tillerson earlier this month on terror financing, but we don't yet know the details of how this agreement would be implemented, and we wait to see the results.

Madam Chairman, it is important to note also, that Saudi Arabia, the UAE, Egypt, and other nations now isolating Qatar, face challenges as well. Two weeks ago, our subcommittee held a similar hearing on our relationship with Saudi Arabia, in which we explored both our strategic partnership as well as our deep concern over Saudi Arabia's slow progress on human rights and continued exporting of fundamentalist ideology.

Today's hearing should not be about determining who is right. Today's hearing should rather make it clear that this fighting among partners does not advance America's interests. We should be pushing for unity among our allies to fight common threats. We should be pushing all of our partners in the region to cut off funding to terror groups. We should be urging every leader to curtail hate speech, and improve the records of human rights, including treating women as equal members of society.

Madam Chairman, I hope that today we can assess our relationship with Qatar thoughtfully. I hope our witnesses can help us unpack how past diplomatic risk between Qatar and its Gulf neighbors can inform our path forward, and I hope that we can review the major demands made on Qatar to reduce relations with Iran, shut down the Turkish military base, sever all ties to terror organizations, including the Muslim Brotherhood, and shut down Al Jazeera to understand the motivations behind these demands, and in an effort to see how a resolution might actually come.

I trust that our witnesses today will lead us in an interesting and worthwhile conversation. And I appreciate—again, I appreciate them being here.

And I yield back the balance of my time.

Ms. ROS-LEHTINEN. Thank you very much, Mr. Deutch.

And now we will turn to our members for any opening remarks they might have, starting with Mr. Cook of California.

Mr. COOK. Thank you, Madam Chair.

This is going to be a very interesting hearing. It is almost similar to the one we had with Turkey. Friend or foe? And, obviously, as already been discussed, some of the issues that are going to come up, the relationship with Hamas, Taliban, financing and everything else, and now there is a new wrinkle, and that is the World Cup and the North Korean workers that are going to be paid for by that government there with the money going back to North Korea that is probably going to be used to finance more missile research. And I don't think I have to tell the panel or anybody here that this is an even more troubling scenario than some of the others. We are talking about a large number of North Koreans, including the North Korean military that are going to be working on that.

And I hope that our panel will also discuss that as well as the other issues that were just raised.

Thank you, Madam Chairman.

Ms. ROS-LEHTINEN. Thank you, sir.

Mr. Suozzi of New York.

Mr. SUOZZI. Suozzi. Thank you so much, Madam Chair.

Ms. ROS-LEHTINEN. Suozzi. I am so sorry.

Mr. SUOZZI. It's okay. I am used to that for a long time now.

Madam Chairman and ranking member, I want to thank you so much for holding this hearing. It is very timely. It is very difficult for many of us to untangle all the complicated relationships that exist in this region. We simply don't have the background that the witnesses do, and that is why we are so appreciative of them being here to testify today.

Between the religious dispute and the tribal and family relationships and the historic disputes and people's economic interests, it is sometimes difficult to untangle who the different parties are. And no one in the region really has clean hands. And we need to figure out how to promote our agenda in America and throughout the West, which is that we have to stand strong and hard against people who use propaganda and hate speech and economic warfare to promote extremism and violence.

So I am excited to be here today and to listen to what the witnesses have to say. Thank you.

Mrs. WAGNER [presiding]. Thank you, gentlemen.

The Chair now recognize Mr. Zeldin for 5 minutes—oh, 1 minute. These are 1 minute that we are doing. Sorry. I have just taken over the chair.

Mr. Zeldin, you are recognized.

Mr. ZELDIN. Well, thank you, Madam Chairwoman. And I am very much looking forward to today's hearing and listening to our witnesses and being able to ask questions and getting feedback.

A lot of great our thoughts are already shared, I especially like the ranking member's opening testimony. He really touched on so much of what I, too, care deeply about.

Recently, I was in Qatar, and I found them to be very welcoming. They were going as far out of their way as possible to make progress in our relationship. We visited the military base that was there, and our servicemembers were well taken care of in a good, strategic location. And at the same exact time, I am greatly concerned by the welcoming atmosphere that exists for Hamas. And I just want to better understand the future of this relationship, and the reasons why the reality exists as it does right now in 2017.

So thank you, again, for doing this hearing. I look forward to the testimony.

Mrs. WAGNER. Thank you, Mr. Zeldin.

The Chair now recognizes Mr. Lieu for 1 minute, please.

Mr. LIEU. Thank you, Madam Chair, and ranking member, for holding this hearing.

There have been a series of allegations between Qatar and the countries who are imposing a blockade, and it is hard for me to figure out what is true and what is false.

But let me say what I do see. I do see a blockade that has resulted in some cruel consequences. From what I have read, you have families now being separated based on national origin, and that to me is highly troubling.

I also see a Trump administration that is sending very mixed signals. At the same time, the Secretary of State is saying de-escalate, do not blockade, you have the President doing the opposite, essentially claiming credit for this blockade. Then you have also the United States sending $12 billion worth of fighter jets to Qatar. I would love to see the panel clarify that, and I want you to tell us not only what our policy toward Qatar should be, but what it actually is right now.

I yield back.

Mrs. WAGNER. The gentleman yields back.

The Chair now recognizes the gentleman from California, Mr. Issa, for 1 minute.

Mr. ISSA. Thank you, Madam Chair.

It seems like only yesterday that the President said, You are either with us or against us. And the world said, oh, it is too simple. But I think as we evaluate Qatar and the other Gulf states, we have to ask that basic question is, is Qatar with us? Are they moving toward being more with us? Are they cooperating? Are they moving toward Iran? Are they moving away from the U.S.?

These are questions that I believe that we are going to be asking today that I am hoping to hear throughout the day, because I believe that although you are either with us or against us, there are shades of gray in all of our allies in the region.

It is clear that Turkey has been moving away from us since 2003. It is clear that Qatar has not been the best of actors when it comes to taking away funding from those who support terrorism, and it is clear that if they are moving with us, we need to have that demonstrated just as we asked Saudi Arabia, the United Arab Emirates and others to demonstrate on a regular basis.

Thank you, Madam Chair. I yield back.

Mrs. WAGNER. The gentleman yields back.

The Chair now recognizes the gentleman from New York, Mr. Meeks, for 1 minute.

Mr. MEEKS. Thank you, Madam Chair.

And I would want to join with the statement of Mr. Lieu. I think what we have to talk about here is the issue of fairness, and we need to make sure, I think, that when you talk about Qatar and the other countries in the region, we as the United States, I don't think, should be picking and choosing. We should be talking, because we need them all, and we need to figure out how we work collectively together.

Qatar has been—I think it is clear, they have shown that they have done some things that have very good for the United States with our military base, trying to make sure that working with us in regards to the war on terror.

And I think what needs to happen here, and especially if you talk about Qatar, we need to bring in as a committee the individuals from both the Bush administration and the Obama administration, because there is deep dialogue and conversation that we could have with them to talk about the region and the people that they have asked, Qatar being one, to do certain things on behalf of the United States. And if that is the case, then those individuals should not be held responsible if they are working cooperatively with us.

So I look forward to hearing the testimony from the witnesses, and I think that we just need to make sure that we have a level playing field here.

Mrs. WAGNER. Thank you, Mr. Meeks, for your opening statement.

We will now turn to our witnesses. I would, first, like to welcome back Mr. Jonathan Schanzer, who is the senior vice president of research for the Foundation for Defense of Democracies. Dr. Schanzer serves as a counterterrorism analyst at the Department of Treasury, and prior to that, worked as a research fellow at the Washington Institute for Near East Policy. Welcome back, Dr. Schanzer.

I would also like to welcome back Dr. Matthew Levitt, who directs the Stein Program on Counterterrorism and Intelligence at the Washington Institute for Near East Policy. Previously, Dr. Levitt served as the Deputy Assistant Secretary for Intelligence and Analysis at the U.S. Department of Treasury, and before that, as an FBI counterterrorism analyst. We are glad to have you back with us today, Dr. Levitt.

Finally, I would like to welcome Ilan Goldenberg, who is a senior fellow and director of the Middle East Security Program at the Center for a New American Security.

Prior to CNAS, Mr. Goldenberg served as the chief of staff of a special envoy for Israeli-Palestinian negotiations at the U.S. Department of State. From 2012 to 2013, Mr. Goldenberg served as a senior professional staff member on the Senate Foreign Relations Committee covering Middle East issues. In that capacity, he acted as one of the lead drafters of the Syria Transition Support Act, which provided additional authorities to arm the Syrian opposition. The bill passed the Senate Foreign Relations Committee in May 2013. And I thank you for being here with us today.

Dr. Schanzer, we will begin with you for your opening statement.

STATEMENT OF JONATHAN SCHANZER, PH.D., SENIOR VICE PRESIDENT, FOUNDATION FOR DEFENSE OF DEMOCRACIES

Mr. SCHANZER. Madam Chairman, Ranking Member Deutch, and members of the subcommittee, on behalf of the Foundation for Defense of Democracies, thank you for the opportunity to testify.

As many of you know, FDD has been producing research and analysis on Qatar since the eruption of the Arab Spring in 2011.

Our critique has been consistent. We have pointed to Qatari support for Hamas, the Taliban, jihadists in Syria, jihadists in Libya and the Muslim Brotherhood. We have been critical of Qatar for the invective broadcast on state-owned Al Jazeera. We have tracked the many reports suggesting that Qatar paid ransom to terrorism groups, and we have noted through the work of my colleague, David Andrew Weinberg, that Qatar has failed to take action against U.S. and U.N.-designated terrorist financiers. In my written testimony, I document these problems, and I am happy to discuss them further. But for a moment, I would like to address how Qatar has responded to the allegations against it.

After ignoring criticism from think tanks like FDD for the better part of a decade, Qatar now claims it is being unfairly singled out. To be sure, the other Gulf countries have their problems. A recent State Department report noted that U.N.-designated terrorist financiers continue to operate in Kuwait; Saudi Arabia continues to finance the spread of Wahhabism; and the entire Gulf suffers from a democracy deficit.

But to understand why Qatar is identified first among Gulf states for terrorism financing, just imagine for a moment that you are a policeman, and you have just watched five cars speed past you going 80 miles per hour. And zooming past them is a red Ferrari going 90 miles an hour. Which car would you pull over? Well, that Ferrari is Qatar. Indeed, Qatar support is overt. It is egregious, and it is brazen.

As the Gulf crisis has dragged on, Qatar has also been defiant, insisting its definition of terrorism differs from that of its critics. This is a particularly poor defense from a country claiming to be an American ally in the war on terrorism. As for the current crisis between Qatar and its neighbors, the Saudis and the Emiratis have been engaged in serious competition with Qatar for years. They attempt to outdo one another through foreign investment, domestic businesses, media interests, lobbying in western capitals, and other soft power.

Since the Arab Spring, however, that rivalry has boiled over. Both sides have thrown their support behind various proxies representing their interests in the Middle East. The Qataris back the Muslim Brotherhood and other Islamist actors, and for their part, the Saudis and the Emiratis are working to preserve the Arab world order, pushing for stability at the expense of the possibility for reform. These two visions of the Middle East are fundamentally at odds with one another.

The wise U.S. policy is not to back one Gulf state or another. We must rather pursue policies ensuring that terrorism financing in the Gulf comes to an end.

I offer you the following suggestions: First, Congress should assess whether Qatar should continue to host Al Udeid, our most significant air base in the Middle East. Fighting our war on terrorism from Qatar sends a convoluted message to our allies in the region.

Congress should work with the Justice Department to ensure that Qatar not only adopts laws to combat terrorism financing, but also fully implements them.

Congress should consider passing the bipartisan Stop Terrorist Operational Resources and Money, or STORM Act, of 2017. The bill, which was introduced in the Senate and not yet in the House, could label Qatar and other countries as Jurisdictions of Terrorism Financing Concern.

Congress should press the State Department, pursuant to the State Department Authorization Act, to issue its report on which States paid ransom to terrorists over the last year. Congress should press for full implementation of the Export Administration Act, subjecting countries like Qatar that host terrorist operatives to certain licensing requirements for dual-use goods.

Congress, of course, must continue to monitor Qatar's neighbors. Indeed, even if Qatar's problems were resolved tomorrow, the Gulf would remain an area of significant concern for terrorism finance.

Finally, I believe it is time we have a frank discussion about Gulf money in Washington. Those who feed from this trough are often unable to engage honestly about the policies and behaviors of their benefactors, even when they fly in the face of U.S. interests. Indeed, I would be curious to hear how many of you have been approached by lobbyists since the Gulf crisis began, let alone in the lead up to today's hearing.

There are issues that I did not address in this testimony. If I miss anything you wish to discuss, I am happy to answer your questions. And on behalf of Foundation for Defense of Democracies, I thank you again for inviting me to testify.

[The prepared statement of Mr. Schanzer follows:]

House Foreign Affairs Committee
Subcommittee on Middle East and North Africa

Assessing the U.S. – Qatar Relationship

JONATHAN SCHANZER

Senior Vice President
Foundation for Defense of Democracies

Washington, DC
July 26, 2017

www.defenddemocracy.org

Jonathan Schanzer   July 26, 2017

Chairman Ros-Lehtinen, Ranking Member Deutch, and distinguished members of the subcommittee, on behalf of the Foundation for Defense of Democracies, thank you for the opportunity to testify. My testimony today will look at the substance behind the current Gulf spat, with a focus on Qatar's support for a range of extremist groups and the grievances that the other Arab states harbor against Qatar. At the end, I will address the question of U.S. military assets in Qatar, as well as several policies that Washington should consider.

Context

Members of the committee, as you know, FDD has been producing research and analysis on Qatar since the eruption of the Arab Spring in 2011. Our critique of Qatari foreign policy has been consistent. We have pointed to Qatari support for Hamas, the Taliban, jihadists in Syria, jihadists in Libya, and the Muslim Brotherhood. We have been critical of the Qataris for the invective that is too often broadcast on state-owned Al-Jazeera. And we have noted through the excellent work of my colleague David Andrew Weinberg that Qatar has failed to take action against numerous U.S.- and UN-designated terrorist financiers living in Qatar.[1]

We have not singled out Qatar. Indeed, we have produced work that is critical of the other Gulf states, such as Saudi Arabia and Kuwait, when it has been warranted. FDD's David Andrew Weinberg testified about Saudi Arabia's troubling educational curriculum before the House Foreign Affairs Committee just last week.[2] But Qatar has been an obvious area of interest in light of its incredibly brazen and open support for terrorist groups designated by the United States.

This support for terrorist groups is particularly disturbing in light of the fact that Qatar is home to the al-Udeid air base, the launch point for thousands of strikes carried out by the U.S. in the war on terrorism. When confronted over its support for extremists, Qatar's response has been lax or dismissive, with little in the way of new commitments or follow-through. The fact is, Qatar has wielded its immense wealth and soft power to undermine U.S. interests, including America's allies in the region.

FDD has worked hard to educate Congress, the executive, and the American public on the challenge of Qatar. We found that the previous administration was generally willing to listen, but was unwilling to redress the problem. Having failed to gain much traction for six years, we decided to hold a conference on U.S. Qatar policy with the arrival of a new administration. We held our event on May 23 here in Washington, DC.[3]

Our conference was, I believe, the first major conference to shine a light on Qatar. It featured current and former officials, figures from both sides of the aisle, who expressed deep concerns

---

[1] David Andrew Weinberg, "Qatar and Terror Finance, Part II: Funders of al-Qaeda in Syria," *Foundation for Defense of Democracies*, January 2017.
(http://www.defenddemocracy.org/content/uploads/documents/11717_Weinberg_Qatar_Report.pdf)
[2] David Andrew Weinberg, "Saudi Arabia's Troubling Educational Curriculum," *Testimony before the House Committee on Foreign Affairs*, July 19, 2017. (http://docs.house.gov/meetings/FA/FA18/20170719/106289/HHRG-115-FA18-Wstate-WeinbergD-20170719.pdf)
[3] "Qatar and the Muslim Brotherhood's Global Affiliates: New U.S. Administration Considers New Policies," *Foundation for Defense of Democracies*, May 23, 2017. (http://www.defenddemocracy.org/events/qatar-and-muslim-brotherhood/)

Jonathan Schanzer   July 26, 2017

about Qatar, its support for extremist groups, and its long-term viability as a U.S. ally if that support continued. Shortly after the conference concluded, we learned that the Qatar News Agency was hacked. The Qatari response intimated that Doha saw our conference as part of a coordinated assault.[4] To be clear: We had nothing to do with it. FDD strongly condemns hacking. Now, according to the *Washington Post*, the U.S. intelligence agency allegedly believes that the UAE was behind the hack against Qatar, although the Emirati ambassador to Washington vehemently denies this.[5]

Several days after the Qatar News Agency hack, the Emirati ambassador was himself hacked. His emails were leaked to journalists worldwide. The U.S. intelligence community has yet to determine who was behind that attack. Several stories emerged featuring emails between my colleagues at FDD and the ambassador. The implication was that we were coordinating our efforts with the UAE or that we take Emirati money.[6] For the record, FDD took no direction from a foreign government. Nor did we take any foreign government money. Although many think tanks engage in this practice, we never have and never will.

The hack and hack-back has since yielded a full-blown spat among the Gulf states. The Gulf and other Arab states cut diplomatic ties with Qatar on June 5, blocking maritime, land, and air routes for both traffic and trade.[7] Qatar's financial ratings have dropped,[8] and its currency has been under strain.[9]

Qatar has been defiant, insisting that its definition of terrorism differs greatly from its critics. Qatar's alternate view of reality and morality is a poor defense. It is reminiscent of the so-called "affluenza" teen who was charged with a drunk driving crash that killed four people, but whose defense team argued that the teen's life of privilege made it difficult for him to determine right from wrong.[10] A country of great wealth, Qatar is now effectively arguing the same thing. But the Qataris fully grasp the list of grievances against them. I will summarize them below.

---

[4] "Qatar faces hostile media campaign, particularly in US: FM," *The Peninsula* (Qatar), May 25, 2017, (https://www.thepeninsulaqatar.com/article/25/05/2017/Qatar-faces-hostile-media-campaign,-particularly-in-US-FM)

[5] Aya Batrawy and Fay Abuelgasim, "Qatar suggests cyberattack emanated from a Gulf neighbor," July 20, 2017, *The Washington Post*, (https://www.washingtonpost.com/world/middle_east/qatar-suggests-cyberattack-emanated-from-gulf/2017/07/20/18522be6-6d64-11e7-abbc-a53480672286_story.html?utm_term=.f4908db5e65a)

[6] Akbar Shahid Ahmed, "Someone Is Using These Leaked Emails To Embarrass Washington's Most Powerful Ambassador," *The Huffington Post*, June 3, 2017, (http://www.huffingtonpost.com/entry/otaiba-ambassador-uae-leaked-emails_us_5932bf04e4b02478cb9bec1c)

[7] "Saudi Arabia, Egypt lead Arab states cutting Qatar ties, Iran blames Trump," *Reuters*, June 5, 2017. (http://www.cnbc.com/2017/06/04/saudi-arabia-bahrain-and-egypt-cut-diplomatic-ties-with-qatar.html)

[8] Alec Macfarlane, "Qatar hit by ratings downgrade over blockade crisis," *CNN*, June 8, 2017, (http://money.cnn.com/2017/06/08/investing/qatar-rating-downgrade/index.html)

[9] Alanna Petroff. "British banks have stopped selling Qatari cash," *CNN*, June 30, 2017 (http://money.cnn.com/2017/06/30/investing/qatar-rival-uk-currency/index.html)

[10] Lisa Maria Garza and Timothy Williams, "Teenager Who Used 'Affluenza' Defense Is Sentenced to Jail," *The New York Times*, April 13, 2016. (https://www.nytimes.com/2016/04/14/us/teenager-who-used-affluenza-defense-is-sentenced-to-jail.html)

Jonathan Schanzer   July 26, 2017

Support for Hamas

Qatar is a top headquarters for Hamas, a Palestinian terrorist group designated by the State Department in 1997.[11] Hamas operatives work out of Qatar with impunity, where they fundraise and even plan terrorist attacks.

When the Syrian civil war forced Hamas leaders like Politburo chief Khaled Meshal to flee, Qatar offered him refuge, along with several other Hamas political leaders now living in Doha.[12] This includes Hamas' spokesman, Ezzat al-Rishq.[13]

Husam Badran, a Hamas terrorist responsible for taking dozens of Israeli lives, has been living in Qatar since 2011 after being released from Israeli prison.[14] According to an Israeli Defense Forces website, Badran directed from Doha a 2013 Hamas plot to kidnap Israeli soldiers.[15] He also was responsible for directing the activities and recruitment for a Hamas headquarters in the West Bank that was broken up in 2015, and from providing that network with hundreds of thousands of dollars from his perch in Qatar.[16] He still appears to be residing in Qatar today.[17]

Hamas military official Saleh Arouri lived for a time in Qatar after being expelled from Turkey (he is now believed to be in Lebanon). Arouri is widely believed to have plotted the abduction and murder of the three Israeli teens in 2014. That event led to a war between Israel and Hamas in the summer of 2014.[18] He is under U.S. sanctions for funding and directing Hamas terror operations,[19] and also stands accused of plotting a Hamas coup against the Palestinian Authority in the West Bank.[20]

[11] U.S. Department of State. "Foreign Terrorist Organizations," accessed July 24, 2017. (https://www.state.gov/j/ct/rls/other/des/123085.htm)

[12] David Andrew Weinberg, "Qatar vs. Saudi Arabia: How Iran and the Brotherhood Tore the Gulf Apart," *The National Interest*, June 8, 2017. (http://nationalinterest.org/feature/qatar-vs-saudi-arabia-how-iran-the-brotherhood-tore-the-gulf-21068)

[13] Jonathan Schanzer and Kate Havard, "By Hosting Hamas, Qatar is Whitewashing Terror," *Newsweek*, May 11, 2017. (http://www.newsweek.com/qatar-hosting-hamas-whitewashing-terror-606750)

[14] David Barnett, "Hamas terrorist in Qatar helps Hebron terror cell plan kidnappings," *FDD's Long War Journal*, January 31, 2013. (http://www.longwarjournal.org/archives/2013/01/israeli_authorities_uncover_ha.php)

[15] "IDF & ISA Uncover Hamas Terrorist Assets in Hebron," *Israeli Defense Forces* (Israel), January 31, 2013. (https://www.idfblog.com/2013/01/31/idf-isa-uncover-hamas-terrorist-assets-in-hebron/)

[16] Yoav Zitun, "Shin Bet arrests 40 Hamas members in Nablus," *Ynet News* (Israel), July 1, 2015. (http://www.ynetnews.com/articles/0,7340,L-4674956,00.html)

[17] See Facebook profile at https://www.facebook.com/profile.php?id=100010044737611&fref=nf.

[18] Jonathan Schanzer, "Time for the US to stop Qatar's support for terror," *New York Post*, April 20, 2017. (http://nypost.com/2017/04/20/time-for-the-us-to-stop-qatars-support-for-terror/)

[19] U.S. Department of the Treasury, Press Release, "Treasury Sanctions Major Hamas Leaders, Financial Facilitators and a Front Company," September 10, 2015. (https://www.treasury.gov/press-center/press-releases/Pages/jl0159.aspx)

[20] Yaakov Lappin, "Hamas in West Bank 'planned to topple Palestinian Authority,'" *The Jerusalem Post* (Israel), August 18, 2014. (http://www.jpost.com/Arab-Israeli-Conflict/Massive-Hamas-infrastructure-in-West-Bank-planned-to-topple-the-Palestinian-Authority-371409)

Jonathan Schanzer   July 26, 2017

Qatar is further believed to be hosting Talal Ibrahim Abd al-Rahman Sharim, a member of Hamas' armed wing, the Izz ad-Din al-Qassam Brigades, who reportedly played a role in financing Hamas cells in the West Bank from Qatari territory.[21]

In 2014, the Kuwaiti daily newspaper *Al-Seyassah* reported that Hamas was moving its financial operations to Qatar.[22] And there is ample evidence to support this. For example, it was reported that "Bakri Hanifa, who is a major financial operative for Hamas ... moved 'tens of millions of dollars' to Turkey from Qatar before being sent onward to Hamas's political and military wings."[23]

Zahir al-Jabareen is another Hamas official who worked out of Qatar to send money from Gulf countries to Hamas."[24]

Maher Ubeid, "a member of Hamas's politburo who reportedly was put in charge of laundering tens of millions of euros from Turkish territory ... to Hamas's military and political wings in Gaza," was also based in Qatar.[25]

Video footage from 2015 showed Mohammed al-Qawasmi, whom *Al-Seyassah* identified as a Hamas official,[26] was allowed to fundraise on state-controlled Qatari television.[27]

According to a leaked cable attributed to former Secretary of State Hillary Clinton, the U.S. government pressed the Qatari government in 2009 on "terror finance related to Hamas."[28] Five years later, former Under Secretary for Terrorism and Financial Intelligence David Cohen noted in 2014 that "Qatar, a longtime U.S. ally, has for many years openly financed Hamas, a group that continues to undermine regional stability."[29] However, Husam Badran told *Al-Monitor* in 2014,

---

[21] Yonah Jeremy Bob, "Shin Bet Busts Palestinian Footballer For Meeting With Hamas Terrorist in Qatar," *The Jerusalem Post* (Israel), June 11, 2014. (http://www.jpost.com/Sports/Palestinian-soccer-player-admits-to-meeting-with-Hamas-operative-while-in-Qatar-356003)

[22] "حماس" تحول أنشطتها المالية من السعودية إلى قطر وتركيا" (Hamas moves Its Financial Network from Saudi Arabia to Qatar and Turkey)," *Al Seyassah* (Kuwait), April 7, 2014. (http://al-seyassah.com/-حماس-تحول-أنشطتها-المالية-من-السعودية/)

[23] Jonathan Schanzer, "Hamas Still Finds Harbor in Turkey," *The Weekly Standard*, June 8, 2016. (www.weeklystandard.com/hamas-still-finds-harbor-in-turkey/article/2002746)

[24] «أبو عارف».. القصة الكاملة للغامض الذي يدير أموال حركة حماس في مصر" (Abu Aref: The Complete Story of the Mysterious Man Who Manages Hamas Movement's Money in Egypt)," *El Mogaz* (Egypt), December 21, 2013. (http://www.elmogaz.com/node/119383)

[25] 40 مليون يورو من تركيا لـ"حماس" لتعزيز سيطرتها على غزة" (40 Million Euros from Turkey to Hamas for Strengthening Its Control over Gaza)," *Palestine Press News Agency* (UK), November 6, 2011. (http://www.palpress.co.uk/arabic/?Action=Details&ID=65344)

[26] مشعل يواجه انتقادات حادة داخل "حماس" بعد اعتقال قطر أحد كوادرها المالية" (Mashal Faces Sharp Criticism inside Hamas after Qatar Arrests One of Its Financial Officers," *Al-Seyassah* (Kuwait), January 28, 2015. (http://al-seyassah.com/-مشعل-يواجه-انتقادات-حادة-داخل-حماس-بعد/)

[27] AlrayyanTV, "برنامج المختصر ـ الحلقة الحاديه و الاربعون - 2014-08-06 (Summary Program - Episode 41 - 2014-08-06)," *YouTube*, August 7, 2014. (https://www.youtube.com/watch?v=mAFcUhncLHE&t=2324s)

[28] "Terrorist Finance: Action Request for Senior Level Engagement on Terrorism Finance," *WikiLeaks Cable: 09STATE131801_a*, accessed July 20, 2017. (https://wikileaks.org/plusd/cables/09STATE131801_a.html)

[29] Under Secretary for Terrorism and Financial Intelligence David Cohen, "Confronting New Threats in Terrorist Financing," *Remarks at the Center for a New American Security*, March 4, 2014. (https://www.treasury.gov/press-center/press-releases/Pages/jl2308.aspx)

Jonathan Schanzer   July 26, 2017

"There is no suspension of the Qatari financial support for the movement, since their relationship is ongoing."[30]

Qatari Support for al-Qaeda in Syria

As a Gulf country seeking to influence the post-Arab Spring politics of the Middle East, Qatar is not unique. However, Qatar's desire to bring down the Assad regime ultimately gave way to backing al-Qaeda in Syria.

As early as 2012, al-Qaeda's Jabhat al-Nusra commanders met with senior Qatari military officials and financiers in Doha.[31] In 2013, certain Qatari weapons shipments to militant groups were winding up in the hands of Jabhat al-Nusra. It was for this reason that the Obama administration requested that Qatar halt the export of heat-seeking shoulder-fired missiles to Syrian militants.[32]

In one very strange episode, a financier named Abd al-Aziz bin Khalifa al-Attiyah reportedly travelled to the Syrian-Lebanese border via Beirut to distribute funds to Jabhat al-Nusra militants. Lebanese authorities arrested him but released him following a Qatari protest. Al-Attiyah is a Qatari sheikh and cousin of former Qatari Foreign Minister Khalid al Attiyah.[33] Upon his return, he received a lifetime achievement award from the Qatar Olympic Committee and appeared in a video for a Syria fundraising campaign with another Qatari who would later be sanctioned by the U.S. for funding al-Qaeda.[34]

Broadly speaking, Qatar has worked to normalize al-Qaeda in Syria. Qatar reportedly promised additional financial backing should Jabhat al-Nusra rebrand and cosmetically distance itself from al-Qaeda.[35] This likely explains the two rebrands of the al-Qaeda affiliate, first as Jabhat Fateh al-Sham (JFS) in July 2016,[36] and again as Hayat Tahrir al-Sham (HTS) in January 2017.[37]

---

[30] Adnan Abu Amer, "Egypt-Qatar rapprochement rattles Hamas." *Al-Monitor*, December 30, 2014. (http://www.al-monitor.com/pulse/originals/2014/12/egypt-qatar-rapprochement-hamas.html)

[31] Jay Solomon and Nour Malas, "Qatar's Ties to Militants Strain Alliance," *The Wall Street Journal*, February 23, 2015. (http://www.wsj.com/articles/qatars-ties-to-militants-strain-alliance-1424748601)

[32] Mark Mazzetti, C. J. Chivers, and Eric Schmitt, "Taking Outsize Role in Syria, Qatar Funnels Arms to Rebels," *The New York Times*, June 29, 2013. (http://www.nytimes.com/2013/06/30/world/middleeast/sending-missiles-to-syrian-rebels-qatar-muscles-in.html)

[33] Jay Solomon and Nour Malas, "Qatar's Ties to Militants Strain Alliance," *The Wall Street Journal*, February 23, 2015. (https://www.wsj.com/articles/qatars-ties-to-militants-strain-alliance-1424748601?tesla=y)

[34] "43 new designations specifically address threats posed by Qatar linked and based Al Qaida Terrorism Support Networks," *Emirates News Agency* (UAE), June 9, 2017. (http://wam.ae/en/details/1395302618259); الشيخ الدكتور وجدي غنيم ~ كلمتي لحملة مدد أهل الشام" (Sheikh Dr. Wagdy Ghoneim - My Speech for the Madad Ahl al-Sham Campaign)," *YouTube*, June 2, 2013. (https://youtu.be/IncUorGGzil?t=11m)

[35] Mariam Karouny. "Insight - Syria's Nusra Front May Leave Qaeda to Form New Entity," *Reuters*, July 19, 2017. (http://uk.reuters.com/article/uk-mideast-crisis-nusra-insight-idUKKBN0M00G620150304)

[36] "Syria war: Who are Jabhat Fateh al-Sham?" *BBC News* (UK), August 1, 2016. (http://www.bbc.com/news/world-middle-east-36924000)

[37] "Tahrir Al-Sham: Al-Qaeda's latest incarnation in Syria," *BBC News* (UK), February 28, 2017. (http://www.bbc.com/news/world-middle-east-38934206)

Jonathan Schanzer   July 26, 2017

Impunity for Designated al-Qaeda Financiers in Qatar

Qatar also has failed to prosecute many of the designated terrorist financiers, primarily al-Qaeda financiers, within its borders. FDD's David Andrew Weinberg has painstakingly documented this.[38]

The problem has also been well documented by successive senior Treasury Department officials. For example, in March 2014, then-Under Secretary for Terrorism and Financial Intelligence David Cohen called Qatar, as well as Kuwait, "permissive jurisdictions" for terrorist finance,[39] and that October, he accused Doha of giving legal impunity to Khalifa al-Subaiy and 'Abd al-Rahman al-Nu'aymi, Qatari nationals under U.S. and UN charges for raising millions of dollars for al-Qaeda. Al-Subaiy was identified as having close ties to 9/11 mastermind Khalid Sheikh Mohammad before the latter's capture in 2003 and had apparently worked as a senior employee at Qatar's central bank.[40]

Cohen's successor at Treasury, Adam Szubin, stated in October 2016 that Qatar "still lacks the necessary political will and capacity to effectively enforce their CFT (combating the financing of terrorism) laws against all terrorist financing threats regardless of organization or affiliation."[41] And in February 2017, the former Assistant Secretary for Terrorist Financing, who had just stepped down, noted that designated terror financiers were still "operating openly and notoriously" in Qatar, as well as Kuwait.[42]

Hajjaj al-Ajmi is one figure who regularly visited Doha to fundraise for Jabhat al-Nusra. He encouraged Qataris to "Give your money to the ones who will spend it on jihad, not aid." The Ministry of Endowment and Islamic Affairs reportedly invited al-Ajmi to speak.[43] The U.S. Treasury designated al-Ajmi as a Jabhat al-Nusra funder in August 2014.[44] According to the UAE, two Qatari nationals based in Qatar helped al-Ajmi with his fundraising there.[45]

---

[38] David Andrew Weinberg, "Qatar and Terrorism Finance, Part II: Private Funders of al-Qaeda in Syria," *Foundation for Defense of Democracies*, January 2017.
(http://www.defenddemocracy.org/content/uploads/documents/11717_Weinberg_Qatar_Report.pdf)
[39] Under Secretary for Terrorism and Financial Intelligence David Cohen, "Confronting New Threats in Terrorist Financing," *Remarks at the Center for a New American Security*, March 4, 2014. (https://www.treasury.gov/press-center/press-releases/Pages/jl2308.aspx)
[40] Robert Mendick, "Terror financiers are living freely in Qatar, US discloses," *The Telegraph* (UK), November 16, 2014. (http://www.telegraph.co.uk/news/worldnews/islamic-state/11233407/Terror-financiers-are-living-freely-in-Qatar-US-discloses.html)
[41] Under Secretary Adam Szubin, "Countering the Financing of Terrorism," *Remarks at The Paul II. Nitze School of Advanced International Studies*, October 20, 2016. (https://www.treasury.gov/press-center/press-releases/Pages/jl0590.aspx)
[42] David Andrew Weinberg, "Terror Financiers 'Operating Openly' in Qatar and Kuwait," *Foundation for Defense of Democracies*, February 14, 2017. (http://www.defenddemocracy.org/media-hit/david-weinberg-terror-financiers-operating-openly-in-qatar-and-kuwait/)
[43] Andrew Gilligan, "The 'Club Med for terrorists,'" *The Telegraph* (UK), September 27, 2014. (http://www.telegraph.co.uk/news/worldnews/middleeast/qatar/11125897/The-Club-Medfor-terrorists.html)
[44] U.S. Department of the Treasury, Press Release, "Treasury Designates Three Key Supporters of Terrorists in Syria and Iraq," August 6, 2014. (https://www.treasury.gov/press-center/press-releases/Pages/jl2605.aspx)
[45] "43 new designations specifically address threats posed by Qatar linked and based Al Qaida Terrorism Support Networks," *Emirates News Agency* (UAE), June 9, 2017. (http://wam.ae/en/details/1395302618259)

Jonathan Schanzer

Another Kuwaiti national, Shafi al-Ajmi, reportedly boasted on Twitter that he raised $52,000 for Jabhat al-Nusra in Qatar. He instructed Qataris to route donations through the Foundation Sheikh Thani Ibn Abdullah for Humanitarian Services (RAF), a Qatari royal charity.[46] The U.S. Treasury designated al-Ajmi as a Jabhat al-Nusra funder in August 2014.[47]

The U.S. Treasury designated Abd al-Rahman bin Umayr al-Nu'aymi for transferring $600,000 to al-Qaeda in Syria.[48] Al-Nu'aymi previously served as an advisor to the Qatari government and founding member of Sheik Eid bin Mohammed al-Thani Charitable Foundation, and he served for a number of years as the chairman of a state-funded Qatari think tank.[49]

The U.S. Treasury designated Hamid Abdullah al-Ali in 2006 for financially supporting al-Qaeda in Iraq.[50] He was added to the UN's al-Qaeda sanctions list as well in 2008, and would have been added sooner but Qatar blocked his designation while it was a member of the Security Council. In 2012, the Ministry of Endowment and Islamic Affairs invited him to deliver a Friday sermon at Doha's Qatar Grand Mosque, in which he extoled the jihad in Syria.[51]

The U.S. Treasury designated Sa'd bin Sa'd Muhammad Shariyan Al-Ka'bi in August 2015 for facilitating terrorist funding social networks and ransom payment benefiting al-Qaeda in Syria.[52] He reportedly still resides in Qatar.[53]

According to the State Department's country reports on terrorism released last week, Qatar never prosecuted and convicted terror financiers before 2015.[54] According to the *Associated Press*, five UN-designated terror financiers have since been prosecuted by Qatar, but for some reason "are not imprisoned."[55] This subcommittee might consider requesting an explanation from Qatar about its justice system relating to terrorist financiers.

---

[46] Andrew Gilligan, "The 'Club Med for terrorists.'" *The Telegraph* (UK), September 27, 2014. (http://www.telegraph.co.uk/news/worldnews/middleeast/qatar/11125897/The-Club-Medfor-terrorists.html)

[47] U.S. Department of the Treasury, Press Release, "Treasury Designates Three Key Supporters of Terrorists in Syria and Iraq," August 6, 2014. (https://www.treasury.gov/press-center/press-releases/Pages/jl2605.aspx)

[48] U.S. Department of Treasury, Press Release. "Treasury Designates Al-Qa'ida Supporters in Qatar and Yemen," December 18, 2013. (https://www.treasury.gov/press-center/press-releases/Pages/jl2249.aspx)

[49] Andrew Gilligan, "The 'Club Med for terrorists,'" *The Telegraph* (UK), September 27, 2014. (http://www.telegraph.co.uk/news/worldnews/middleeast/qatar/11125897/The-Club-Medfor-terrorists.html)

[50] U.S. Department of the Treasury, Press Release, "Treasury Designations Target Terrorist Facilitators," December 7, 2006. (https://www.treasury.gov/press-center/press-releases/Pages/hp191.aspx)

[51] Andrew Gilligan, "The 'Club Med for terrorists,'" *The Telegraph* (UK), September 27, 2014. (http://www.telegraph.co.uk/news/worldnews/middleeast/qatar/11125897/The-Club-Medfor-terrorists.html)

[52] Samuel Rubenfeld, "U.S. Targets Alleged Qatari Financiers of Terrorism," *The Wall Street Journal*, August 5, 2015. (https://blogs.wsj.com/riskandcompliance/2015/08/05/u-s-targets-alleged-qatari-financiers-of-terrorism/); U.S. Department of the Treasury, Press Release, "Treasury Designates Financial Supporters of Al-Qaida and Al-Nusrah Front," August 5, 2015. (https://www.treasury.gov/press-center/press-releases/Pages/jl0143.aspx)

[53] Yaya J. Fanusie and Alex Entz, "Al-Qaeda's Branch in Syria: Financial Assessment," *Foundation for Defense of Democracies*, June 2017. (http://www.defenddemocracy.org/content/uploads/documents/CSIF_TFBB_AQIS.pdf)

[54] U.S. Department of State, "Chapter 2. Country Reports: Middle East and North Africa," *Country Reports on Terrorism 2016*, July 2017. (https://www.state.gov/j/ct/rls/crt/2016/272232.htm)

[55] Aya Batrway, "Qatar crisis raises questions about defining terrorism," *Associated Press*, July 7, 2017. (https://apnews.com/de239a64452f402ca6e08a0e734c347a/Qatar-crisis-raises-questions-about-defining-terrorism)

Jonathan Schanzer
July 26, 2017

Kidnapping for Ransom

Qatar has repeatedly been accused of paying ransoms to terrorists. Former Libyan leader Moammar Qaddafi often engaged in this practice as a means to send funds to terrorist groups under legitimate cover.[56] Of course, Qatar's government denies this.[57] But FDD has identified eighteen different episodes in the last six years in which Qatar was reported as a participant in hostage talks.[58]

In 2012 and 2013, Qatar and Oman were accused by sources cited by the *New York Times* and *Wall Street Journal* of paying roughly $20 million in ransoms for European hostages held by al-Qaeda in Yemen.[59] In 2013, *McClatchy* cited a Lebanese security official saying that Qatar paid a ransom for Lebanese pilgrims and Turkish pilots, the former of which was reportedly held by al-Qaeda in Syria.[60] In 2014, the *Wall Street Journal* reported that Qatar paid a $16 million ransom for Syrian nuns held by al-Qaeda in Syria.[61] The same year, Qatar reportedly paid $25 million to Jabhat al-Nusra for the release of 45 Fijian UN peacekeepers kidnapped near the Golan Heights.[62] Qatar also was accused of facilitating a ransom to al-Qaeda related to the release of U.S. journalist Peter Theo Curtis, according to sources cited by the *Daily Beast*.[63] In 2015, Qatar was accused by Lebanese and Syrian sources of paying $25 million as part of a hostage deal Doha mediated between al-Qaeda's Nusra Front and Beirut for kidnapped Lebanese security officials.[64]

According to a source quoted by the *Financial Times*, "ransom payments are the straw the broke the camel's back" leading up to the current Gulf crisis with Qatar. That piece cited sources alleging that in April, Qatar had paid up to a billion dollars for the release of its citizens, including members of Qatar's royal family, who had been taken hostage by an Iraqi terrorist group. The sources stated that Qatar had given $200-$300 million to Sunni jihadists in Syria who were holding hostages, with most of the money going to Hayat Tahrir al-Sham. Another $700 million reportedly went to

---

[56] Jonathan Schanzer, "Terrorism's Back Door," *Los Angeles Times*, August 26, 2003. (http://articles.latimes.com/2003/aug/26/opinion/oe-schanzer26)

[57] Peter Kovessy," Foreign minister: Qatar does not pay ransoms," *Doha News* (Qatar), September 30, 2014. (https://dohanews.co/foreign-minister-qatar-pay-ransoms/)

[58] David Andrew Weinberg, "Qatar and Terrorism Finance, Part II: Private Funders of al-Qaeda in Syria," *Foundation for Defense of Democracies*, January 2017. (http://www.defenddemocracy.org/content/uploads/documents/11717_Weinberg_Qatar_Report.pdf)

[59] Rukmini Callimachi, "Paying Ransoms, Europe Bankrolls Qaeda Terror," *The New York Times*, July 29, 2014. (https://www.nytimes.com/2014/07/30/world/africa/ransoming-citizens-europe-becomes-al-qaedas-patron.html?_r=1); Ellen Knickmeyer, "Al Qaeda-Linked Groups Increasingly Funded by Ransom," *The Wall Street Journal*, July 29, 2014. (https://www.wsj.com/articles/ransom-fills-terrorist-coffers-1406637010)

[60] Mitchell Prothero, "Lebanese pilgrims held for year by Syrian rebels back in Beirut," *McClatchy*, October 19, 2013. (http://www.mcclatchydc.com/news/nation-world/world/article24757552.html)

[61] Ellen Knickmeyer, "Al Qaeda-Linked Groups Increasingly Funded by Ransom," *The Wall Street Journal*, July 29, 2014. (https://www.wsj.com/articles/ransom-fills-terrorist-coffers-1406637010)

[62] "Report: UN Had Qatar Pay Off Al-Qaida Fighters for Release of Fiji Peacekeepers," *Haaretz* (Israel), October 11, 2014. (http://www.haaretz.com/middle-east-news/1.620228)

[63] Shane Harris, "US Pays Off Hostage Takes," *The Daily Beast*, April 29, 2015. (http://www.thedailybeast.com/us-pays-off-hostage-takers)

[64] David Andrew Weinberg, "Wrong Way: The Problem With Al Qaeda Prisoner Swaps," *The National Interest*, January 4, 2016. (http://nationalinterest.org/feature/wrong-way-the-problem-al-qaeda-prisoner-swaps-14794)

Jonathan Schanzer   July 26, 2017

the Iranian-backed bloc in the region, with $300 million going to IRGC-backed Shiite militias in Iraq and Tehran taking a $400 million cut.[65]

Support for the Taliban

In December 2009, the State Department listed Qatari cooperation on terrorism finance among "the worst in the region," noting that, "the Taliban … and other terrorist groups exploit Qatar as a fundraising locale."[66] In 2010, members of the Taliban reportedly began to arrive in Qatar to establish an official presence. In 2012, the Taliban established a political office in Qatar to "spread understanding with the international community."[67] When the Obama administration began its dialogue in 2013 with the Taliban, Qatar permitted the group to open a diplomatic office in Doha.[68]

The Taliban presence increased further with a May 2014 Qatari-facilitated prisoner swap[69] involving Bowe Bergdahl, an American soldier captured by the Taliban after "wandering off an American outpost in the Paktika province in June 2009,"[70] in exchange for five Taliban figures with "high-ranking positions in Mullah Omar's organization" and "noteworthy connections to Al Qaeda."[71] The Taliban Five were released to Qatar "in coordination with the Qatari government, which pledged to enforce a temporary travel ban and provided assurances the men would not pose a threat to the US."[72]

Troubling questions have been raised about the extent to which Qatar is monitoring or politicking the activities of the Taliban Five. *Fox News* reported in 2015 that "at least three of the five Taliban leaders … have tried to plug back into their old terror networks."[73] Reports indicate that at least one of the former Taliban detainees may have been in contact with fighters from the Afghan terror group in January 2015 and encouraged attacks on U.S. forces.[74] A top fundraiser for the Haqqani

---

[65] Erica Solomon, "The $1bn hostage deal that enraged Qatar's Gulf rivals," *Financial Times* (UK), June 5, 2017. (https://www.ft.com/content/dd033082-49c9-11e7-a3f4-c742b9791d43?segmentid=acce4131-99c2-09d3-a635-873e61754ec6)

[66] "US fears on Taliban cash revealed," *Al-Jazeera* (Qatar), December 6, 2010. (http://www.aljazeera.com/news/middleeast/2010/12/20101251936167112.html)

[67] Thomas Joscelyn, "Afghan Taliban announces new 'political office' in Qatar," *FDD's Long War Journal*, January 3, 2012. (http://www.longwarjournal.org/archives/2012/01/afghan_taliban_annou.php)

[68] Paul Alster, "Qatar's terror funding makes it more foe than friend to U.S., critics say," *Fox News*, September 16, 2014. (http://www.foxnews.com/world/2014/09/16/qatar-cozies-up-to-us-while-funding-terror-say-critics/)

[69] Thomas Joscelyn, "Sgt. Bowe Bergdahl exchanged for top 5 Taliban commanders at Gitmo," *FDD's Long War Journal*, May 31, 2014. (http://www.longwarjournal.org/archives/2014/05/sgt_bowe_bergdahl_ex.php)

[70] Thomas Joscelyn, "Taliban touts Bergdahl swap as key 'achievement,'" *FDD's Long War Journal*, April 22, 2016. (http://www.longwarjournal.org/archives/2016/04/taliban-touts-bergdahl-swap-as-key-achievement.php)

[71] Thomas Joscelyn, "Afghan peace council reportedly seeks talks with Taliban commanders held at Gitmo," *FDD's Long War Journal*, March 17, 2011. (http://www.longwarjournal.org/archives/2011/03/afghan_peace_council_1.php)

[72] Jeremy Diamond, "House report accuses Obama of violating law in Bergdahl exchange," *CNN*, December 10, 2015. (http://www.cnn.com/2015/12/09/politics/taliban-5-bowe-bergdahl-congress-report/index.html)

[73] Catherine Herridge, "Official: At least 3 members of 'Taliban 5' tried to reconnect with terror networks," *Fox News*, March 25, 2015. (http://www.foxnews.com/politics/2015/03/25/official-at-least-3-members-taliban-5-trying-to-reconnect-with-terror-networks.html)

[74] Spencer Ackerman, "One of 'Taliban Five' in Bowe Bergdahl swap allegedly returned to militancy," *The Guardian* (UK), January 30, 2015. (http://www.theguardian.com/world/2015/jan/30/taliban-five-bowe-bergdahl-swap-return-militancy)

group was purportedly able to fly to Qatar, meet one or more of the five men, and fly out before he was captured in a third country.[75]

According to one Afghan official recently cited by the *New York Times*, "Doha is now is home to about 100 Taliban officials and their relatives, who live comfortably at Qatari state expense."[76]

Under fire in recent weeks for its support of terrorist groups, the government in Doha insists that it hosted the Taliban with the permission, or even encouragement, of the Obama administration.[77] This may have been the case. But that does not mean that Qatar has upheld its end of the bargain. It also does not mean that the office has helped achieve U.S. objectives. One senior U.S. official told me earlier this year that he heard repeatedly from Afghan officials that the Taliban office in Doha directly undermined the Afghan government.[78] This committee might consider investigating whether the Taliban presence in Qatar ultimately helps or hurts our interests.

Support for Libyan Islamists

On June 5, 2017, Libya's eastern-based government joined other Arab countries in cutting ties with Qatar, with Foreign Minister Mohammed al-Deri asserting that Doha was "harboring terrorism."[79] The move reflected a longstanding frustration with Qatar's sponsorship of Islamist extremists in the war-torn country. Since the 2011 revolution, Libya has been the site of a Gulf proxy war. The UAE, Saudi Arabia, and Egypt have backed the eastern-based government and Khalifa Haftar's Libyan National Army (LNA). By contrast, Qatar, Sudan, and Turkey have backed the Tripoli-based Presidency Council/Government of National Accord.

Qatar's interference in Libya dates to the revolution against the Qaddafi regime, when Doha provided robust support to the rebels.[80] Since then, Qatar has reportedly sent massive amounts of weapons to Islamist militants battling the Western-backed government in Libya.[81] A March 2013 UN report noted that in 2011 and 2012, Qatar violated the UN arms embargo by "providing military material to the revolutionary forces through the organization of a large number of flights and the deliveries of a range of arms and ammunition."[82] And according to the *Libya News Agency*,

[75] Margherita Stancati and Ehsanullah Amiri, "Haqqani Leaders Detained in Persian Gulf, Not Inside Afghanistan," *The Wall Street Journal*, October 19, 2014.
(https://www.wsj.com/articles/haqqani-leaders-detained-in-persian-gulf-not-inside-afghanistan-1413733878)
[76] Declan Walsh, "Qatar Opens Its Doors to All, to the Dismay of Some," *The New York Times*, July 16, 2017.
(https://www.nytimes.com/2017/07/16/world/middleeast/doha-qatar-blockade.html)
[77] Qatar hosted Taliban 'at request of US government,'" *Al-Jazeera* (Qatar), June 11, 2017.
(http://www.aljazeera.com/news/2017/06/qatar-hosted-taliban-request-government-170611114833584.html)
[78] Conversation with U.S. official, April 28, 2017.
[79] "Libya government cuts relations with Qatar," *Economic Times* (India), June 5, 2017.
(http://economictimes.indiatimes.com/news/international/world-news/libya-government-cuts-relations-with-qatar/articleshow/59004515.cms)
[80] David Roberts, "Behind Qatar's Intervention in Libya," *Foreign Affairs*, September 28, 2011.
(https://www.foreignaffairs.com/articles/libya/2011-09-28/behind-qatars-intervention-libya)
[81] Feras Bosalum and Ayman al-Warfalli, "Libyan PM accuses Qatar of sending planes with weapons to Tripoli," *Reuters*, September 15, 2014. (http://uk.reuters.com/article/2014/09/14/uk-libya-security-qatar-idUKKBN0H90WE20140914)
[82] United Nations Security Council, "Final report of the Panel of Experts established pursuant to resolution 1973 (2011) concerning Libya," March 9, 2013. (http://www.securitycouncilreport.org/atf/cf/%7B65BFCF9B-6D27-4E9C-8CD3-CF6E4FF96FF9%7D/s_2013_99.pdf); Karim Mezran and Elissa Miller, "Resolving the Gulf crisis

Jonathan Schanzer   July 26, 2017

Doha has provided more than 750 million euros to extremist groups in Libya since 2011.[83] Arab officials I spoke to believe that these deliveries of arms and cash arrive to Western Libya by way of a commercial airline that is owned by Qatar.[84]

According to Kristian Coates Ulrichsen of the Baker Institute for Public Policy, "Qatar developed close links with key Islamist militia commanders [in Libya] such as Abdelhakim Belhadj, once the head of the Libyan Islamic Fighting Group and, in 2011, the commander of the Tripoli Brigade."[85] According to Arab officials, Belhadj was the Libyan apostle of Osama bin Laden who maintained close and continuing ties to Qatar.[86] Belhadj launched Hizb al-Watan in 2012,[87] which Arab officials believed have maintained close ties to LIFG and received continued support from Qatar.[88]

Ulrichsen also notes the connection between Qatar and "Ismael al-Salabi, the leader of one of the best-supplied rebel militias, the Rafallah al-Sahati Companies. Qatar was widely suspected of arming and funding al-Salabi's group, whose sudden munificence of resources in 2011 earned it the nickname of the 'Ferrari 17 Brigade.'"[89]

Ismael al-Salabi's brother, Ali al-Salabi, is a prominent Libyan cleric close to the emir of Qatar. One Egyptian source claims that he maintains close ties to the LIFG.[90] This is a claim echoed by Arab officials familiar with the situation in Libya.[91]

On June 8, 2017, the LNA held a press conference alleging proof of Qatar's malign role in Libya. The LNA charged that Qatari intelligence General Salim Ali al-Jarboui supported al-Qaeda, the Islamic State, and the Muslims Brotherhood by transferring $8 billion from the Qatari Tunisian National Bank to the Housing Bank of Tataouine Governorate in southern Tunisia. According to the LNA, Qatar supported the assassination of senior officials, facilitated training of Islamist extremists by Hamas, and helped transport Libyan Islamists to Syria. Mesmari also presented a letter by Mohammed Hamad Al Hajri, acting charge d'affaires at the Qatar Embassy in Libya, supporting the notion that Qatar had deployed military units to the country.[92]

---

through Libya," *The Hill*, July 1, 2017. (http://thehill.com/blogs/pundits-blog/foreign-policy/340089-resolving-the-gulf-crisis-through-libya)

[83] "Qatar's support to terrorist groups in Libya 'will not pass without charge': Hafter." *Egypt Independent*, June 1, 2017. (http://www.egyptindependent.com/qatar-support-terrorist-groups-libya/)

[84] Interview with Arab officials, Summer 2017.

[85] Kristian Coates Ulrichsen, *The United Arab Emirates: Power, Politics and Policymaking*, (London and NY: Routledge, 2017), page 197.

[86] Interview with Arab officials, Summer 2017.

[87] Katerina Nikolas, "Libya's Abdel Hakim Belhaj to launch Hizb al-Watan Islamic party," *Digital Journal*, May 24, 2012. (http://www.digitaljournal.com/article/325423)

[88] Interview with Arab officials, Summer 2017.

[89] Kristian Coates Ulrichsen, *The United Arab Emirates: Power, Politics and Policymaking*, (London and NY: Routledge, 2017), page197.

[90] "Ali Mohamed Mohamed Al-Salabi: Tamim's man in Libya," June 11, 2017. (http://www.albawabaeg.com/93180)

[91] Interview with Arab officials, Summer 2017.

[92] "Libyan army provides documentary proof of Qatar's crimes in country," *Al-Arabiya* (UAE), June 9, 2017. (https://english.alarabiya.net/en/News/north-africa/2017/06/09/Libyan-army-provides-documentary-proof-of-Qatar-s-crimes-in-country-.html); Andrew McGregor, "Qatar's Role in the Libyan Conflict: Who's on the Lists of Terrorists and Why," *The Jamestown Foundation*, July 14, 2017. (https://jamestown.org/program/qatars-role-libyan-conflict-whos-lists-terrorists/)

Jonathan Schanzer   July 26, 2017

When Saudi Arabia, the UAE, Bahrain, and Egypt issued a "terrorist list" of 59 individuals and 12 entities linked to Qatar, it included one entity (the Benghazi Defense Brigades) and five individuals from Libya.[93] On June 12, the LNA released a second list of 75 Libyan individuals and 9 organizations tied to Qatar.[94] One highlight of the first list includes Al-Sadiq Abd al-Rahman Ali al-Ghiryani, who previously served the Grand Mufti of Libya, who has called for the destruction of the eastern government.[95]

The Muslim Brotherhood

Much of the current conflict between Qatar and its neighbors can be traced back to Qatari support for the Muslim Brotherhood. The Muslim Brotherhood's presence in Qatar dates back to 1974, when students studying in countries like Kuwait and Egypt returned and wanted to form their own chapter of the organization. Since then, Qatar has hosted the movement's leaders and supported its regional activities, particularly since the eruption of the Arab Spring.[96] That was when Qatar began to actively support Muslim Brotherhood branches in Egypt, Libya, Syria, Tunisia, and beyond.[97]

In Libya, Doha became the first Arab government to recognize the National Transitional Council (NTC) as the only legitimate representation of the people. It provided military and financial support to the rebels fighting against Moammar Qaddafi and created a pro-revolutionary channel that balanced Qaddafi's propaganda. Some Libyans, however, like the former NTC Deputy Prime Minister Ali Tarhouni, suspected that Qatar was providing support to the Brotherhood.[98]

Qatar invested $18 billion in Egypt shortly after Morsi's election to support his Brotherhood regime, and it reportedly supplied funds to the Islamist Tunisian Nahda Party, as well.[99] It also backed the Brotherhood-dominated Syrian National Council, founded in late 2011, despite other Arab states' hesitation.[100]

Al-Jazeera

---

[93] "Saudi Arabia, UAE and Egypt issue Qatar-linked terrorism list," *The National* (UAE), June 9, 2017. (https://www.thenational.ae/world/saudi-arabia-uae-and-egypt-issue-qatar-linked-terrorism-list-1.51035)
[94] "HoR promotes hatred and violence with list of 'terrorists' says Libya's Uganda ambassador; full list published," *Libya Herald*, June 12, 2017. (https://www.libyaherald.com/2017/06/12/hor-promotes-hatred-and-violence-with-list-of-terrorists-says-libyas-uganda-ambassador-full-list-published/)
[95] Andrew McGregor, "Qatar's Role in the Libyan Conflict: Who's on the Lists of Terrorists and Why," *The Jamestown Foundation*, July 14, 2017. (https://jamestown.org/program/qatars-role-libyan-conflict-whos-lists-terrorists/)
[96] "Shedding light on the Qatari-Muslim Brotherhood connection," *The Arab Weekly* (UK), July 9, 2017. (http://www.thearabweekly.com/Highlights/8808/Shedding-light-on-the-Qatari-Muslim-Brotherhood-connection)
[97] Hanin Ghaddar, "Qatar Bets on Islamists," *Woodrow Wilson International Center for Scholars*, February 7, 2013. (https://www.wilsoncenter.org/article/qatar-bets-islamists)
[98] Ibid.
[99] Jonathan Schanzer and David Andrew Weinberg, "How Saudi Arabia and Qatar are the Tortoise and the Hare of the Middle East," *The Atlantic*, August 27, 2013. (https://www.theatlantic.com/international/archive/2013/08/how-saudi-arabia-and-qatar-are-the-tortoise-and-the-hare-of-the-middle-east/279090/)
[100] Ibid.

Qatar's Arab neighbors are also deeply concerned about the broadcasts of Qatar-owned Al-Jazeera. Some of the concerns are shared here in Washington, as well.

After the Egyptian coup against Mohammed Morsi, Al-Jazeera hosted exiled Brotherhood leaders at a five-star hotel in Doha and gave them airtime to advocate for their cause. Al-Jazeera also heavily aired the Brotherhood's protests against the new Egyptian government.[101]

The channel has a long history of incitement to violence, biased reporting, supporting Islamist ideologies, and acting as a tool of the Qatari government. I do not believe that the demand issued by the UAE, Saudi Arabia, Bahrain, and Egypt to shut down Al-Jazeera is realistic.[102] But I do believe Qatar needs to do more to ensure that the content on this state-backed channel is addressed.

For example, in Syria, the channel has provided a platform to presenters who call for violence against Alawites. One host, Faisal al-Qassem, said of Alawites: "The Alawites don't need demonization, they are demons, even Satan, the Devil himself, is ashamed of them."[103]

Additional criticisms of Al-Jazeera include its reference to suicide bombers as "martyrs" and the Islamic State as "the state organization."[104] The channel has hosted figures who advocate for political Islam as well as more radical ones from al-Qaeda and Hezbollah who call for jihad.[105] One of the London Bridge bombers, Youssef Zaghba, reportedly was inspired by Al-Jazeera.[106]

Al-Jazeera's reporting on Israel has been consistently egregious. Recently, the network's English affiliate reported on "three Palestinians killed," omitting the fact that they were armed with guns and shot two Israeli police officers to death before being killed.[107] The network's Arabic station

---

[101] Eric Trager, "The Muslim Brotherhood Is the Root of the Qatar Crisis," *The Atlantic*, July 2, 2017. (https://www.theatlantic.com/international/archive/2017/07/muslim-brotherhood-qatar/532380/)

[102] Naser Al Wasmi, "UAE: Al Jazeera has gone beyond incitement to hostility and violence," *The National* (UAE), July 19, 2017. (https://www.thenational.ae/world/uae-al-jazeera-has-gone-beyond-incitement-to-hostility-and-violence-1.530768)

[103] "The Media's War: How the press is fueling Syria's conflict," *Syria Justice and Accountability Centre*, October 31, 2016. (https://syriaaccountability.org/updates/2016/10/31/the-medias-war-how-the-press-is-fueling-syrias-conflict/)

[104] Graham Ruddick, "Al-Jazeera: the Qatar broadcaster at centre of diplomatic crisis," *The Guardian* (UK), June 24, 2017. (https://www.theguardian.com/media/2017/jun/24/al-jazeera-the-qatar-broadcaster-at-centre-of-diplomatic-crisis)

[105] Ben Lynfield, "Al Jazeera Journalists Urge Israel Not to Close Bureau," *The Jerusalem Post* (Israel), June 13, 2017. (http://www.jpost.com/Israel-News/Politics-And-Diplomacy/Al-Jazeera-Journalists-urge-Israel-not-to-close-bureau-496754)

[106] "How Qatar's Al Jazeera promoted extremism and violence," *Gulf News* (UAE), July 12, 2017. (http://gulfnews.com/news/gulf/qatar/qatar-crisis/how-qatar-s-al-jazeera-promoted-extremism-and-violence-1.2057646)

[107] "Al Jazeera fails to mention attack as it reports on 'three killed Palestinians,'" *Ynet News* (Israel), July 14, 2017. (http://www.ynetnews.com/articles/0,7340,L-4989220,00.html)

Jonathan Schanzer   July 26, 2017

went further, calling the three assailants "martyrs."[108] Al-Jazeera Arabic does this virtually every time a Palestinian is killed in the act of attacking Israeli civilians or armed forces.[109]

Al-Jazeera has often featured Yousuf al-Qaradawi, the spiritual leader of the Muslim Brotherhood, who called the Holocaust "divine punishment," and has advocated on air for killing Jews.[110]

In Israel's most recent war with Hamas in 2014, Al-Jazeera Arabic's reporting mirrored Hamas' directives to observers on how to report on the conflict. The network followed Hamas' instructions to describe Palestinians as "martyrs" or "victims" of "Israeli oppression." Al-Jazeera called all Palestinian casualties "innocent civilians," even if they were known combatants.[111]

During the Iraq War, Al-Jazeera received criticism for airing videos by al-Qaeda's leadership, who called for violence against the U.S. and its allies. It promoted the Islamist ideology of groups like al-Qaeda by describing suicide bombings as "paradise operations" and terrorist activities as acts of "resistance."[112] In April 2013, Iraq suspended the licenses of Al-Jazeera due to accusations of incitement. At that point, more than 170 people had been killed due to sectarian fighting, which the Communication and Media Commission attributed in part to Al-Jazeera's reporting. The regulatory group argued that the sectarian language used in their reporting created "criminal acts of revenge by attacking the security forces."[113]

These, of course, are just a few representative examples of the controversial material aired on Al-Jazeera.

The Current Gulf Crisis

Qatar's neighbors are justified in their concern about the aforementioned policies, particularly if their interests are in a stable Middle East. Yet, Qatar's Gulf neighbors are certainly not free from guilt. Based on conversations I have had with current and former Treasury officials, Kuwait ranks among the top terror finance concerns in the Gulf, alongside Qatar. According to the State Department's Country Reports on Terrorism for 2016, which were released last week, "a number of UN-designated terrorist financiers continued to operate in Kuwait."[114]

---

[108] "استشهاد فلسطيني وإصابة جنديين إسرائيليين بعملية دهس بالخليل" (Martyrdom of a Palestinian and Injuring of Two Israeli Soldiers in Car-Ramming Operation in Hebron)," *Al Jazeera* (Qatar), July 18, 2017. (http://www.aljazeera.net/amp/news/arabic/2017/7/18/استشهاد-فلسطيني-واصابة-جنديين-اسرائيليين-بعملية-دهس-بالخليل)

[109] "مقتل شرطيين إسرائيليين في عملية القدس" (Killing of Two Israeli Police in al-Quds Operation)," *Al-Jazeera* (Qatar), April 14, 2017. (http://mubasher.aljazeera.net/news/القدس-عملية-في-إسرائيليين-شرطيين-مقتل)

[110] "How Qatar's Al Jazeera promoted extremism and violence," *Gulf News* (UAE), July 12, 2017. (http://gulfnews.com/news/gulf/qatar/qatar-crisis/how-qatar-s-al-jazeera-promoted-extremism-and-violence-1.2057646)

[111] David Andrew Weinberg, Oren Adaki, and Grant Rumley, "The Problem with Al Jazeera," *The National Interest*, September 10, 2014. (http://nationalinterest.org/feature/the-problem-al-jazeera-11239?page=show)

[112] Osama Heikal, "Qatar's Dangerous Al Jazeera Backing is Indefensible," *Newsweek*, July 18, 2017. (http://www.newsweek.com/qatars-dangerous-defense-al-jazeera-indefensible-637460)

[113] "Iraq Suspends Al Jazeera, Others, Accusing Them of Inciting Violence," *Reuters*, April 28, 2013. (http://www.huffingtonpost.com/2013/04/28/iraq-al-jazeera-others-inciting-violence_n_3173848.html)

[114] U.S. Department of State, "Chapter 2. Country Reports: Middle East and North Africa," *Country Reports on Terrorism 2016*, July 2017. (https://www.state.gov/j/ct/rls/crt/2016/272232.htm)

Jonathan Schanzer   July 26, 2017

Saudi Arabia continues to finance institutions that teach Wahhabi Islam and also foments religious incitement, thereby ensuring continued radicalization of Muslim youth. And all of the Gulf states suffer from a significant democracy deficit.

To understand the current crisis, it is important to understand that the Saudis and the Emiratis have been engaged in a rather ruthless competition with Qatar for years. These three countries have wielded their immense wealth in an attempt to outdo one another through soft power by way of foreign investment, domestic businesses, media interests, lobbying in Western capitals, and more. In the wake of the Arab Spring, as noted above, they began to throw their support behind various proxies representing their interests in the Middle East. Over the last six years, the rivalry has boiled over.

Right now, Qatar's opponents say that Doha has broken its agreement, signed in November 2013, in which signatories pledged not to intervene in the internal affairs of other Gulf states, not to support the Muslim Brotherhood, and not to back opposition groups in Yemen. A second agreement also included provisions ensuring the stability of Egypt. The Gulf states say that Doha has given support to Hezbollah as well as the Muslim Brotherhood in Egypt.[115] The Gulf states recalled their ambassadors temporarily from Doha in protest in March 2014.[116]

Through Kuwaiti mediation, the countries signed the Riyadh Agreement in April, and then an extension of the Riyadh Agreement in November, which led to the reinstatement of the ambassadors and the GCC summit being held, as initially planned, in Doha.[117]

But Qatar's Arab neighbors are unsatisfied with Qatar's track record. Doha continues to support the aforementioned terrorist groups and extremists. Their focus has been on the Muslim Brotherhood, but Qatar has also failed to end the impunity of terror financiers and to stop promoting the ideology that underpins extremist groups, as it pledged it would do under the U.S.-led Jeddah Communiqué of September 2014.[118]

Yet, the grievances run deeper. As far back as 2009, Abu Dhabi's crown prince complained to the U.S. officials that Qatar is "part of the Muslim Brotherhood." Other UAE officials privately described Qatar as "public enemy number 3," after Iran and the Brotherhood.[119]

Tensions escalated dramatically in the wake of the Arab Spring. In 2012, Yusuf Qardawi criticized the UAE on Al-Jazeera, leading to a diplomatic spat with Qatar. Tensions worsened when the UAE arrested a number of Emirati members of the Muslim Brotherhood, a group known as the Association for Reform and Guidance (Jamiat al-Islah wa Tawjih). That crackdown was followed by the arrest of eleven Egyptians on January 1, 2013 who were suspected of being members of the

---

[115] Jim Sciutto and Jeremy Herb, "The secret documents that help explain the Qatar crisis," *CNN*, July 11, 2017. (http://www.cnn.com/2017/07/10/politics/secret-documents-qatar-crisis-gulf-saudi/index.html)
[116] Jay Solomon and Nour Malas, "Qatar's Ties to Militants Strain Alliance," *The Wall Street Journal*, February 23, 2015. (http://www.wsj.com/articles/qatars-ties-to-militants-strain-alliance-1424748601)
[117] Habib Toumi, "GCC endured its worst diplomatic crisis in 2014," *Gulf News* (UAE). December 27, 2014. (http://gulfnews.com/news/gulf/saudi-arabia/gcc-endured-its-worst-diplomatic-crisis-in-2014-1.1432568)
[118] The Jeddah Communique, September 11, 2014. (https://2009-2017.state.gov/r/pa/prs/ps/2014/09/231496.htm)
[119] James M. Dorsey, "Wahhabism vs. Wahhabism: Qatar challenges Saudi Arabia," *M.E. Transparent*, July 25, 2014. (http://inetranspcm.cluster011.ovh.net/spip.php?page=article&id_article=28932&var_lang=en&lang=en)

Muslim Brotherhood and conspiring to destabilize the UAE. It was then learned that several Emirati members of Al-Islah had escaped a crackdown in the UAE and found refuge in Qatar.[120] In 2014, recordings acquired by Libyan rebels and subsequently posted to YouTube exposed the former emir of Qatar discussing with Moammar Gaddafi a plan to undermine and even overthrow the Saudi royal family.[121]

Most recently, reports have surfaced alleging that Qatar informed al-Qaeda of a military operation in Yemen, resulting in a suicide bomb attack that left Emirati troops injured. "Our Qatari allies informed al-Qaeda of our precise location and what we were planning to do. We then received four suicide bombers at our door," UAE ambassador to Russia Omar Saif Ghobash told BBC.[122] Other claims, conveyed by Arab officials, suggest that Qatar may have also shared similar information with Iran-backed Houthi fighters and forces loyal to Ali Abdullah Saleh in Yemen, also directly leading to Emirati and Saudi deaths.[123]

In other words, there are deeper reasons Saudi Arabia, the UAE, Bahrain, and Egypt decided to cut ties with Qatar on June 5. The Arab states released a list of thirteen demands that included severing ties with the Brotherhood and Hamas, the Palestinian arm of the Brotherhood.[124] But even if Qatar complied, additional challenges would remain.

The Al-Udeid Air Base and Camp As Sayliyah

Remarkably, despite the aforementioned Qatari support for jihadist groups, Qatar hosts America's most significant base in the Middle East: al-Udeid Air Base. The dissonance between American and Qatari policy is palpable. George W. Bush administration officials openly questioned this arrangement,[125] as have Obama administration officials.[126]

Those pushing for a tougher line with Qatar, however, have met with stiff resistance from the U.S. military. Since 2001, Qatar has hosted a significant portion of the U.S. military's forces and equipment in the Gulf.[127] Al-Udeid is home to a large number of the U.S. Air Force's forward deployed strike, logistic, and intelligence assets, which conduct over 15,000 missions per year.[128]

---

[120] Kristian Coates Ulrichsen, *The United Arab Emirates: Power, Politics and Policymaking*, (London and NY: Routledge, 2017), pages 189-203.

[121] Faisal J. Abbas, "Qatar's 'Small State Syndrome,'" *The Huffington Post*, March 9, 2013. (http://www.huffingtonpost.com/faisal-abbas/qatars-small-state-syndro_b_4924001.html)

[122] "Qatar 'informed' al-Qaeda bombers says UAE diplomat," *BBC New* (UK), July 20, 2017. (http://www.bbc.com/news/av/world-middle-east-40673529/qatar-informed-al-qaeda-bombers-says-uae-diplomat)

[123] Interview with Arab official, July 21, 2017.

[124] Asa Fitch, Nicolas Parasie, and Margherita Stancati, "Saudi Arabia, U.A.E., Bahrain and Egypt Cut Diplomatic Ties With Qatar," *The Wall Street Journal*, June 5, 2017. (https://www.wsj.com/articles/saudi-arabia-bahrain-and-uae-cut-diplomatic-ties-with-qatar-1496633817)

[125] Interviews with two Bush administration officials, May 2015.

[126] Jay Solomon and Nour Malas, "Qatar's Ties to Militants Strain Alliance," *The Wall Street Journal*, February 23, 2015. (http://www.wsj.com/articles/qatars-ties-to-militants-strain-alliance-1424748601)

[127] Adam Schreck, "Coalition contributions hailed as vital, even as US handles most air strikes against IS," *Associated Press*, March 13, 2015. (https://www.usnews.com/news/world/articles/2015/03/12/in-coalition-of-many-us-air-power-does-the-heavy-lifting)

[128] U.S. Air Force, 379th Air Expeditionary Wing, "Al Udeid Air Base: Newcomers Guide," August 2015. (http://www.afcent.af.mil/Portals/82/379thAEWimages/2015%20Visitor%20Welcome%20Guide_August.pdf)

Nearby Camp As Sayliyah houses a major U.S. Army staging area and prepositioned stocks called Area Support Group-Qatar (ASG-Qatar).[129] Qatar also hosts the major command centers for U.S. and allied forces for the region, including CENTCOM's forward headquarters and the state-of-the-art Combined Air and Space Operations Center (CAOC).

Qatar sees the U.S. presence on its soil as a significant asset. Following the first Gulf War, when Qatar realized how susceptible it was to regional aggression, the country's leaders sought closer defense ties to the United States. In 1992, the U.S. and Qatar signed a bilateral defense agreement granting America substantial access to facilities in Qatar.[130] As part of the deal, Qatar agreed to invest $1 billion to build al-Udeid Air Base.[131] Doha, which was operating only about a dozen combat aircraft at the time,[132] welcomed the presence of the United States military to bolster its security. According to diplomatic cables, Qatar annually pays for 60 percent of al-Udeid's "upkeep costs."[133]

During the invasion of Iraq and subsequent operations there, thousands of sorties were flown from al-Udeid. As of August 2015, the base hosted the U.S. Air Force's 379th Air Expeditionary Wing – the largest expeditionary air wing in the world.[134] U.S. B-1 bombers, originally stationed at the base to provide air support in Afghanistan, dropped nearly a third of all coalition weapons on the Islamic State targets in Iraq and Syria from al-Udeid until they were rotated home in January 2016. Aerial refueling tankers and surveillance aircraft are still a constant presence at al-Udeid.[135]

The U.S. signed a 10-year defense cooperation agreement with Qatar in December 2013 to allow the U.S. to continue operating and stationing troops at al-Udeid through 2024.[136] But this should not bind the United States. It is incumbent upon Washington to assess whether there are opportunities to operate out of regional countries more aligned with American goals and values.

Such a move is not unprecedented. Once the most vital U.S. air installation in the region, Saudi Arabia's Prince Sultan Air Base supported 5,000 troops and 200 aircraft at its peak.[137] The U.S. in 2003 decided to move its assets to al-Udeid. The move was prompted by a number of factors, including the Saudi refusal to allow American aircraft to launch strikes from the base during the

[129] U.S. Army Central, "ASG-Qatar Facts." February 9, 2015, accessed via Wayback Machine July 24, 2017. (http://web.archive.org/web/20150317233745/http://www.arcent.army.mil/about-us/fact-sheets/asg-qatar)
[130] United States Senate Committee on Foreign Relations, "The Gulf Security Architecture: Partnership with the Gulf Cooperation Council," June 19, 2012. (http://www.foreign.senate.gov/imo/media/doc/746031.pdf)
[131] Christopher M. Blanchard, "Qatar: Background and U.S. Relations," *Congressional Research Service*, January 30, 2014, pages 5-8. (http://fas.org/sgp/crs/mideast/RL31718.pdf)
[132] "Qatar: Military Breakdown," *Military Edge*, October 26, 2014. (http://militaryedge.org/countries/qatar/)
[133] Jack Khoury, "WikiLeaks Cables: Qatar Okays Use of Airbase for U.S. Attack on Iran," *Haaretz* (Israel), November 30, 2010. (http://www.haaretz.com/news/diplomacy-defense/wikileaks-cables-qatar-okays-use-of-airbase-for-u-s-attack-on-iran-1.328081)
[134] U.S. Air Force, 379th Air Expeditionary Wing, "Al Udeid Air Base Newcomers Guide," August 2015. (http://www.afcent.af.mil/Portals/82/379thAEWimages/2015%20Visitor%20Welcome%20Guide_August.pdf)
[135] Robert Burns and Adam Schreck, "Tiny Qatar Plays Outsize Role in U.S. War Strategy," *Associated Press*, September 15, 2014. (http://www.armytimes.com/article/20140915/NEWS08/309150052/Tiny-Qatar-plays-outsize-role-U-S-war-strategy)
[136] "Qatar Signs Defense Accord with U.S.," *Reuters*. December 10, 2013. (http://www.nytimes.com/2013/12/11/world/middleeast/qatar-signs-defense-accord-with-us.html)
[137] "Prince Sultan Air Base," *Global Security*, May 7, 2011. (http://www.globalsecurity.org/military/facility/prince-sultan.htm)

Jonathan Schanzer

July 26, 2017

second Iraq War.[138] But in the end, the Saudis at the time were uncomfortable with the presence of American forces on their soil.

Just as the United States started building a backup CAOC in Qatar when its access to Saudi territory was become more tenuous, now would be the right time to begin thinking about a similar move. At the very least, it would give the U.S. sufficient latitude to get tougher on Doha when it misbehaves.

Below are some options:

Al-Dhafra, UAE: This base sits less than 20 miles southeast of Abu Dhabi.[139] Al-Dhafra has a number of attributes that make it a suitable location. With al-Dhafra only about 200 miles from al-Udeid, U.S. forces would retain the ability to quickly respond to crises throughout the Persian Gulf region. The base is also closer to the strategic Strait of Hormuz in the event of Iranian attempts to block the vital channel.

Al-Dhafra's capacity and value to U.S. operations is evident by the fact that in the first months of the campaign against the Islamic State in the fall of 2014, more coalition strike missions into Syria and Iraq were launched from the base than any other in the region.[140] Additionally, the base is regarded as the busiest in the world for U.S. Air Force surveillance missions.[141] Other missions conducted from al-Dhafra include: bombing missions into Afghanistan, air patrols over the Gulf, and logistics and ISR flights supporting operations throughout the Central Command area of responsibility.[142] The U.S. holds the base and its partnership with the UAE in such high regard that al-Dhafra is used to host some of the U.S.'s most secretive and advanced aircraft, including being one of the few foreign-owned bases to host F-22 stealth fighter deployments.[143]

Shaheed Mwaffaq (Mwaffaq Salti) Air Base, Jordan: This base has played a prominent role in the battle against the Islamic State. The base is located in Azraq, eastern Jordan, and was first used by U.S. aircraft in 1996 to support the no-fly zones over Iraq. Today, Mwaffaq supports a range of

[138] Don Van Natta Jr., "Last American Combat Troops Quit Saudi Arabia," _The New York Times_, September 22, 2003. (http://www.nytimes.com/2003/09/22/international/middleeast/22SAUD.html)

[139] "Al-Dhafra Air Base, UAE," _Global Security_, May 7, 2011. (http://www.globalsecurity.org/military/facility/dhafra.htm)

[140] Rajiv Chandrasekaran, "In the UAE, the United States Has a Quiet, Potent Ally Nicknamed 'Little Sparta,'" _The Washington Post_, November 8, 2014. (http://www.washingtonpost.com/world/national-security/in-the-uae-the-united-states-has-a-quiet-potent-ally-nicknamed-little-sparta/2014/11/08/3fc6a50c-643a-11e4-836c-83bc4f26eb67_story.html)

[141] Tara Copp, "Air Force part of the 'more' for Islamic State fight, Carter says," _Stars and Stripes_, April 17, 2016. (https://www.stripes.com/news/middle-east/air-force-part-of-the-more-for-islamic-state-fight-carter-says-1.404911#.WNkl9G8rJeM)

[142] Rajiv Chandrasekaran, "In the UAE, the United States Has a Quiet, Potent Ally Nicknamed 'Little Sparta,'" _The Washington Post_, November 8, 2014. (http://www.washingtonpost.com/world/national-security/in-the-uae-the-united-states-has-a-quiet-potent-ally-nicknamed-little-sparta/2014/11/08/3fc6a50c-643a-11e4-836c-83bc4f26eb67_story.html)

[143] Amy Butler and Robert Wall, "UAE-Based F-22s a Signal to Iran," _Aviation Week_, April 26, 2012. (http://aviationweek.com/defense/uae-based-f-22s-signal-iran)

Jonathan Schanzer   July 26, 2017

coalition aircraft striking the Islamic State.[144] The base has two runways capable of accommodating all aircraft in the U.S. inventory.

A number of coalition partners have deployed aircraft to Jordan to support the fight against the Islamic State. Both the UAE and Bahrain deployed there to benefit from the country's proximity to the battlefield.[145] France, Belgium, and the Netherlands also deployed fighters to Jordan to conduct strikes within Iraq.[146]

In short, Mwaffaq is an ideal forward base geographically, and its facilities are robust, enabling a full spectrum of missions. No less important, Jordan is an eager partner in the fight against the Islamic State and its politics as a moderate Arab state are crucial for coalition building.

Shaikh Isa Air Base, Bahrain: This is a relatively small air base; it has only one runway and limited ramp space. However, during the first Gulf War, as many as 250 Marine and Navy combat aircraft and 17,500 servicemen made use of the base.[147] It continued to support U.S. operations in the region during the 1990s, hosting F-15s and F-16s flying missions during Operation Southern Watch.[148] After the September 11 attacks, Bahrain permitted U.S. aircraft to fly combat missions out of the base to both Afghanistan and Iraq. The base additionally served as a key logistics hub, moving equipment for the U.S. "surge" in Iraq and operations in Afghanistan.[149] Most recently, the base hosted U.S. Marine Corps AV-8 Harriers and F/A-18 Hornets conducting strike missions against the Islamic State inside Iraq.[150]

---

[144] Douglas Jehl, "Jordan Allowing U.S. to Use Its Air Base for Flights Over Iraq," *The New York Times*, April 9, 1996. (http://www.nytimes.com/1996/04/09/world/jordan-allowing-us-to-use-its-air-base-for-flights-over-iraq.html)

[145] Adam Schreck, "From Jordan Base, UAE Resumes Airstrikes on Islamic State," *Associated Press*, February 10, 2015. (https://japantoday.com/category/world/from-jordan-base-uae-resumes-airstrikes-on-islamic-state); "Bahrain Deploys Warplanes to Jordan for War Against IS," *Agence France Presse*, February 16, 2015. (http://news.yahoo.com/bahrain-deploys-warplanes-jordan-war-against-094504678.html)

[146] Janene Van Jaarsveldt, "Final Netherlands F-16s Headed to Jordan, ISIS Fight," *NL Times* (Netherlands), October 3, 2014. (http://www.nltimes.nl/2014/10/03/final-netherlands-f-16s-headed-jordan-isis-fight/); "France to Send 6 Mirage Jets to Jordan Against Islamic State," *Agence France-Presse*, November 26, 2014. (http://www.defensenews.com/article/20141126/DEFREG04/311260043/France-Send-6-Mirage-Jets-Jordan-Against-Islamic-State); "Belgium to offer fighter jets for ISIS strikes," *Agence France-Presse*, September 24, 2014. (http://english.alarabiya.net/en/News/middle-east/2014/09/24/Belgium-to-offer-fighter-jets-for-ISIS-strikes-.html)

[147] Kenneth Katzman, "Bahrain: Reform, Security, and U.S. Policy," *Congressional Research Service*, April 13, 2017, page 6. (https://fas.org/sgp/crs/mideast/95-1013.pdf)

[148] Office of Assistant Secretary of Defense. "Air Expeditionary Force to Deploy to Bahrain," August 26, 1997. (http://fas.org/news/iraq/1997/08/b08261997_bt439-97.html)

[149] Tech. Sgt. Kevin Nichols, "Mission Complete: Isa Air Base Wraps Up M-ATV Surge," *U.S. Air Force, 379th Air Expeditionary Wing*, October 15, 2010. (http://www.afcent.af.mil/News/tabid/117/Article/350626/mission-complete-isa-air-base-wraps-up-m-atv-surge.aspx)

[150] Richard Whittle, "SP-MAGTF Commander Details ISIL Strikes; Notes 1st Marines 'Could Clear' Iraq," *Breaking Defense*, May 20, 2015. (http://breakingdefense.com/2015/05/past-magtf-commander-details-isil-air-strikes-notes-1st-marines-could-clear-iraq/); Megan Eckstein, "U.S. Marine Corps F/A-18 Hornet Pilot Killed in Crash in England," *USNI News*, October 21, 2015. (http://news.usni.org/2015/10/21/u-s-marine-corps-fa-18-hornet-pilot-killed-in-crash-in-england)

Jonathan Schanzer   July 26, 2017

Bahrain has expressed interest in keeping a long-term American presence to ensure its own security. The monarchy approved NATO E-3 airborne warning and control system (AWACS) and U.S. Navy surveillance aircraft to be stationed at Shaikh Isa in 2010.[151]

With Bahrain, of course, there are drawbacks. In response to the outbreak of the Arab Spring in 2011, Bahrain's government cracked down brutally on demonstrators, resulting in the U.S. halting certain security aid to the country until June 2015.[152] The forecast for future instability in Bahrain prompted further concerns from U.S. lawmakers, who requested in 2015 that the Defense Department explore alternative locations in the Gulf.[153] Additionally, Shaikh Isa is relatively small and not designed to serve as a major air force installation.

Irbil International Airport, Iraqi Kurdistan: The Kurdish Regional Government (KRG), which maintains a long and warm relationship with the United States, controls this facility. The airport hosts two runways. The longer runway, at 4,800 meters (15,700 feet), is one of the longest runways in the world.[154] The facility is large enough to service the largest aircraft in U.S. military service (the C-5 Galaxy) and commercial service (the AN-225).[155] The Irbil airport reportedly serves as a CIA station, which has expanded in recent years, and hosts a U.S. Combat Search and Rescue (CSAR) unit as of February 2015.[156]

However, with passenger and cargo traffic on the rise, there is potential for competition for limited resources.[157] Moreover, the airport's close proximity to Irbil, a major population center, raises operational security concerns that non-military personnel could observe sensitive American military activity and relay that intelligence to hostile forces.

I am happy to provide members of this subcommittee FDD's full assessment of the bases in the region. But it is important to be clear: We should not undertake such a move without carefully studying the alternatives. On the other hand, the time for starting to seriously evaluate our options is now.

---

[151] Walter Pincus, "State Department Cables Detail U.S. Links to Bahrain," *The Washington Post*, February 22, 2011. (http://www.washingtonpost.com/wp-dyn/content/article/2011/02/21/AR2011022103251_pf.html)
[152] "US Lifts Hold on Military Aid to Bahrain," *Agence France-Presse*, June 29, 2015. (http://gulfnews.com/news/gulf/bahrain/us-lifts-hold-on-military-aid-to-bahrain-1.1543177)
[153] Julian Pecquet, "Bahrain Bristles at Threat to Move 5th Fleet," *Al Monitor*, May 18, 2015. (http://www.al-monitor.com/pulse/originals/2015/05/bahrain-fifth-fleet-relocation-bill-threat.html)
[154] "Old & New," *Erbil International Airport*, accessed December 1, 2014. (http://erbilairport.com/ABUT01/F_ABUT01_02_05.aspx)
[155] "AN-225 Mriya Basic Performance," *Antonov Company*, 2014. (http://www.antonov.com/aircraft/transport-aircraft/an-225-mriya/an-225-performance); Australia Defense Forces. 1st Joint Public Affairs Unit, Press Release, "Delivery of Military Stores to Erbil in Northern Iraq Continues," September 17, 2014. (https://www.facebook.com/1stJointPublicAffairsUnit/photos/a.714169595338605.1073742116.349246661830902/714170705338494/)
[156] Mitchell Prothero, "Expansion of 'secret' facility in Iraq suggests closer U.S.-Kurd ties," *McClatchy*, July 11, 2014. (http://www.mcclatchydc.com/news/nation-world/world/article24770413.html); Jack Moore, "U.S. Stations Black Hawks in Kurdish Capital to Ire of Baghdad," *Newsweek*, February 6, 2015. (http://www.newsweek.com/washington-stations-black-hawks-kurdish-capital-ire-baghdad-304916)
[157] "Airport Statistics," *Erbil International Airport*, accessed July 23, 2017. (http://erbilairport.com/ABUT01/F_ABUT01_02_06.aspx)

Jonathan Schanzer   July 26, 2017

Should the U.S. redeploy assets from its bases in Qatar, it must be done in such a way that meets all the U.S. military's operational needs. One existing base may not be able to completely absorb all the manpower and assets. Indeed, dispersing U.S. assets across existing installations in the region could provide permanent solutions.

In the end, the Pentagon still may not wish to rebalance its assets in the Middle East. Should that be the case, the Pentagon will certainly have its reasons, and many of them may not be made public. But it is nevertheless valuable to ascertain whether other bases could better serve American interests. The House Armed Service Committee, Government Accountability Office, or the Congressional Budget Office have the opportunity to explore the strategic and budgetary costs of repositioning American forces in the region. Assessments and hearings would help air American concerns, and allow U.S. decision makers to gain a better understanding of the current challenges and opportunities. Above all, this exercise could send a message to our partners in Doha that our counterterrorism policies and strategic goals should align if they wish to continue cooperating.

Additional Policy Recommendations

The news that Qatar has reportedly agreed to the insertion of two Department of Justice officials in its public prosecution office[158] is a step in the right direction as a result of the external pressure on Qatar as a result of the current Gulf crisis. The real question is whether there will be additional prosecutions and enforcement, and enough political will in Doha to empower prosecutors to go after all relevant suspects in terrorism-related cases. Congress should exercise oversight of the DOJ in this respect, as well as over Qatar's record in choosing and pursuing such cases.

More to the point, as Qatar takes steps to issue decrees and implement laws relating to terrorism and terrorism finance, it should be lauded. But it is the implementation of those laws and regulations that matter most. Qatar's efforts to combat terrorism finance must yield results. Congress should monitor those results.

To that end, Congress should also consider legislation that stipulates closer oversight of Qatar terror finance. Until now, the specific challenges associated with terrorism finance in Qatar have been largely a private, bilateral matter. It may be time to increase the public profile of this problem. One way to do this is through the Stop Terrorists Operational Resources and Money (STORM) Act of 2017, which was introduced in the Senate but not yet in the House. The bill would authorize the president to designate a country that is not adequately combating terrorism financing as a "Jurisdiction of Terrorism Financing Concern." Qatar would almost certainly qualify.[159]

Congress should also press the State Department, pursuant to the State Department Authorization Act, to issue its report on which states paid ransoms to terrorists over the last year.[160] Congress

---

[158] Tom Finn and Sylvia Westall. "U.S. to deploy officials in Qatar in counter-terrorism accord: sources," *Reuters*, July 20, 2017. (https://www.reuters.com/article/us-gulf-qatar-usa-idUSKBN1A51ZD)

[159] David Andrew Weinberg, "Fifteen years since pivotal executive order, STORM Act could help fight terror finance," *The Hill*, September 23, 2016. (http://thehill.com/blogs/congress-blog/homeland-security/297342-fifteen-years-since-pivotal-executive-order-storm-act)

[160] Department of State Authorities Act, Fiscal Year 2017, Pub. L. 114-323, codified as amended at 114 U.S.C. §709. (https://www.congress.gov/bill/114th-congress/senate-bill/1635/text#toc-H8AE3FB2BCCA84E0C8463DCEBF33B2642)

Jonathan Schanzer   July 26, 2017

should further press for full implementation of the Export Administration Act, requiring countries like Qatar that host terrorist operatives to be subject to certain licensing requirements for dual-use goods we would not want falling into terrorists' hands.[161]

Moreover, even though Qatar remains the most brazen of the Gulf states in its support for terrorist groups, Congress must continue to monitor Qatar's neighbors. Indeed, even if Qatar's problems were resolved tomorrow, the Gulf would remain an area of major concern in the area of terrorism finance.

Finally, it is time to face the fact that there is simply too much Gulf money sloshing around in Washington. The Qataris have invested untold millions in think tanks and universities, not to mention lobbyists and other influencers, and they are not the only ones. Qatar's Gulf neighbors are also major players in this game. The end result is that those who feed from this trough are unable to engage in an honest conversation about the policies and behaviors of their benefactors – even when they fly in the face of U.S. interests. Indeed, policymakers have all but given up on the human rights violations, democracy deficits, and terrorism finance challenges associated with this troubled region. Nowhere is that more glaring than with Qatar. I would therefore argue that even an honest conversation here in Congress about the problem would represent a significant step forward.

Members of the committee, there are many issues that I did not address in this testimony. If I have missed anything you wish to discuss, I am happy to answer your questions.

On behalf of the Foundation for Defense of Democracies, I thank you again for inviting me to testify.

---

[161] Export Administration Act of 1979, Pub. L. 108-458, 93 Stat. 503, codified as amended at 96 U.S.C. (http://legcounsel.house.gov/Comps/eaa79.pdf)

Mrs. WAGNER. Thank you, Dr. Schanzer.

Dr. Levitt, you are recognized for your opening statement.

STATEMENT OF MATTHEW LEVITT, PH.D., DIRECTOR AND FROMER-WEXLER FELLOW, STEIN PROGRAM ON COUNTER-TERRORISM AND INTELLIGENCE, THE WASHINGTON INSTITUTE FOR NEAR EAST POLICY

Mr. LEVITT. Thank you, Madam Chairman, Ranking Member Deutch, members of the subcommittee. Thank you for the opportunity to appear before you and assess the U.S.-Qatar relationship and Qatari counterterrorism efforts to date.

Qatar has been a long-time ally of the United States and hosts the largest U.S. military base in the Middle East. But the U.S. has also long criticized the Qatari Government for its lax counterterrorism policies; in particular, shortcomings regarding efforts to combat terror financing.

Moving forward, it is critical to bring this Gulf crisis to a close, and the best way to do that would be to find face saving but substantive and verifiable ways for Qatar to address the most serious shortcomings in its counterterrorism and counter extremism posture. Some of the recent accusations made against Qatar are exaggerated, but many of the claims against Qatar are substantive and focus on long-simmering issues that Doha should have addressed a long time ago.

In recent years, Qatar has maintained an open-door policy for a wide range of Islamist extremism groups from Hamas to the Taliban and others. Most disturbing, however, is the tolerance for fundraising in support for al-Qaeda's Syria branch, Al-Nusra. While Qatar has made previous efforts to halt terror financing, the efficacy of these efforts is questionable.

For example, in 2014, the State Department credited Qatar with shutting down Saad al-Kaabis online fundraising platform for al-Qaeda and Syria called Madad Ahl al-Sham. But the following year, the U.S. Treasury designated Al-Kaabi, who was still operating as a financial supporter of al-Qaeda and al-Qaeda-Syrian affiliate, the Al-Nusra front. Al-Kaabi came up again in the context of a 2017 designation of a Kuwait-based terror financier, Mohammad al-Anizi. Evidently, Al-Kaabi continued to provide funding for Nusra even after Qatar supposedly shut down its fundraising platform in 2014, 3 years earlier, putting a pretty big question mark over the integrity of Qatar's measures to stop terror financing.

Doha has been particularly sketchy on the issue of the prosecution of terrorism financiers in Qatari courts. According to the State Department's 2015 country reports, Doha had made efforts to prosecute significant terrorist financiers. As of 2016, Qatar had prosecuted five terrorist financiers: Ibrahim al-Bakr, Saad al-Kaabi, Abd al-Latif al Kawari, Abd al-Rahman al-Nuaymi, and Khalifa al-Subaiey

It is now clear that of these, two were acquitted, one was convicted but acquitted on appeal, and one was convicted in absentia. As a result, none were in jail when the current inter-Gulf spat broke out. The ones still resident in Qatar are reportedly under surveillance.

According to recent reports, some new arrests may have been made since the current crisis began, likely involving some of those previously tried in Qatari courts. Qatar's lack of transparency about these cases led to much speculation about the country's commitment to these cases. And it is worth noting that just recently, the director of the Qatari Government communications office said, and I quote, "All individuals with links to terrorism Qatar have been prosecuted," which would mean that the total number of suspects is five, which is not the case.

Let me give you just a couple of examples of this odd history. This would have been the second time that Ibrahim al-Bakr was convicted following his 2000 arrest, in which he was subsequently released from prison after he promised not to do terrorist activity in Qatar.

Or consider Khalifa al-Subaiey, who was originally arrested in January 2008 in Bahrain for financing terrorism, undergoing terrorist training, facilitating the travel of others abroad to receive terrorist training and more.

He was arrested again in March 2008 by Qatar and served a 6-month term in prison. He was supposedly under surveillance after he was released. But in 2015, the U.N. Committee on Al-Qaida Sanctions updated his listing with new information, which is no small matter, because it required a new vote of the full U.N. Security Council, and reported that al-Subaiey had resumed terrorist activity.

According to the committee, "After his release, al-Subaiey reconnected with al-Qaeda financiers and facilitators in the Middle East and resumed organizing funds and support of al-Qaeda."

It is important to note that while terror finance prosecutions are difficult cases and acquittals are part of a normally functioning justice system, these are not the only tools available for Qatari officials to deal with financiers effectively serving as regional bundlers of terror funding from donors throughout the region to al-Qaeda and Syria in particular.

The first big test for Qatar will be to populate the domestic designation list just created by Qatar's Emir and to put people on that list.

The U.S. just signed an MOU on counter terror financing with Qatar. It created a whole bunch of new authorities. These authorities need to be implemented in full.

Qatar has a history of past counterterrorism and counterterrorism-related laws in 2004, 2006, 2010, 2014. They were either not implemented, or not implemented in full, and so, therefore, this time, we have to make sure that these are done and done effectively.

Moving forward, the most important thing is that Qatar populates this designation list in a transparent manner, starting with those individuals already designated by the U.S. Treasury and United Nations, who remain at large, and may be continuing to fund and provide material support to al-Qaeda and other terrorist groups.

There are several other recommendations I make in my written statement. I thank you again for the opportunity to testify before you today, and look forward to answering any questions you may have.

[The prepared statement of Mr. Levitt follows:]

Assessing the U.S.-Qatar Relationship

Dr. Matthew Levitt
Fromer-Wexler Fellow and Director, Stein Program on Counterterrorism and Intelligence,
The Washington Institute for Near East Policy

Testimony submitted to the House Foreign Affairs Subcommittee on the Middle East and North Africa
July 26, 2017

Chairman Ros-Lehtinen, Ranking Member Deutch, and members of the MENA subcommittee, thank you for this opportunity to appear before you and assess the U.S.-Qatar relationship and Qatari counter terrorism efforts to date.

Qatar has been a longtime ally of the United States and hosts the largest U.S. military base in the Middle East. However, the U.S. has also long criticized the Qatari government for its lax counterterrorism policies, and in particular shortcomings regarding efforts to combat terrorist financing. Since early June, a coalition of four Arab nations—Saudi Arabia, the UAE, Egypt and Bahrain—has cut off diplomatic and trade relations with Qatar over what they describe as Doha's "financing, adopting, and sheltering extremists."[1] The Qatar crisis has been exacerbated by conflicting statements coming out of the Trump administration, and threatens to undermine the sense of shared mission to counter terrorism that was the intended purpose of the recent Riyadh summit. Moving forward, it is critical to bring this Gulf crisis to a close and the best way to do that would be to find face-saving but substantive and verifiable ways for Qatar to address the most serious shortcomings in its counterterrorism and counter-extremism posture.

Some of the recent accusations made against Qatar are exaggerated, blown out of proportion, or simply not based on fact—consider the release today of a documentary by a UAE-funded media outlet alleging Qatari involvement in the September 11 attacks.[2] But many of the claims against Qatar are substantive and focus on long-simmering issues that Doha should have addressed a long time ago. I will address some of these today.

In recent years, Qatar has housed leaders from Hamas, the Muslim Brotherhood, and the Taliban, and has also provided a platform for extremist leaders to spread their ideology through shows on Al-Jazeera.[3] In 2014, then-Treasury Under Secretary of Terrorism and Financial Intelligence David Cohen reported that Qatar has openly financed Hamas for many years, and continues to contribute to regional instability. Cohen also noted that Qatar has supported other extremist groups operating in Syria. "To say the least," he concluded, "this threatens to aggravate an already volatile situation in a particularly dangerous and

---

[1] "Saudi Arabia Statement on Severing Qatar Ties," *National*, June 5, 2017, https://www.thenational.ae/world/saudi-arabia-statement-on-severing-qatar-ties-1.77960.

[2] Bethany Allen-Ebrahimian, "New UAE Documentary Claims Qatar Complicit in 9/11 Attacks," *Foreign Policy*, July 24, 2017, http://foreignpolicy.com/2017/07/24/new-uae-documentary-claims-qatar-complicit-in-911-attacks-gulf-crisis-saudi-arabia-doha/?utm_content=buffer969b5&utm_medium=social&utm_source=twitter.com&utm_campaign=buffer.

[3] Declan Walsh, "Qatar Opens Its Doors to All, to the Dismay of Some," *New York Times*, July 16, 2017, https://www.nytimes.com/2017/07/16/world/middleeast/doha-qatar-blockade.html.

unwelcome manner."[4] While Cohen recognized that Qatar had made previous efforts to address terrorist financing, he called on the government in Doha to continue working with the U.S. to combat terrorist financing and, in particular, to deal with the ongoing solicitation of donations that fund extremist insurgents under the guise of humanitarian work. According to Cohen, this phenomenon had become increasingly popular.

Although in the past two weeks Qatar has signed a memorandum of understanding on combating terror finance with the U.S. and also reformed its 2004 anti-terrorism law, there are still many of measures that the Qatari government should take to seriously combat terrorism. Qatar's new law allows for the creation of a national designation list, but it was published without an annex of persons or entities to be designated under that authority. Qatar should populate that list, in a transparent manner, starting with those individuals already designated by the U.S. Treasury and the United Nations who remain at large and may be continuing to fund and provide material support to al-Qaeda and other extremist groups. Qatar must continue to take steps to hold these individuals responsible, as well as impose and follow through with comprehensive legislation that will prevent terrorist activity within and outside of its borders.

Qatar's Open-Door Policy

Qatar has welcomed in members of many extremist groups such as Hamas, al-Qaeda, and the Afghan Taliban, acting as a safe-haven and providing a platform for terrorist incitement. For example, for the past few years, Khaled Meshal, who stepped down as the senior leader of Hamas this past May, has been living in Doha.[5] Meshal, a U.S.-designated terrorist, served as the overall leader of Hamas for 21 years, and sought refuge in Qatar after moving around many Arab capitals. In June, media reports claimed that Qatar was expelling Hamas officials from the country as a result of "external pressures," and apologized for the move.[6] While is it not clear who pressured Qatar, or if the Qatari government even asked Hamas leaders to leave, the announcement came just two weeks after President Trump met with leaders in Saudi Arabia, calling on them to jointly address Islamist extremism in the Gulf. It is unknown whether Meshal was among those deported, however, and Qatari Foreign Minister Dr. Khalid bin Mohammed Al Attiyeh called Meshal "a dear guest of Qatar."[7] Beyond Mishal, Qatar also hosted several Hamas operatives involved in planning and directing terrorist attacks, including Salah al-Arouri and others who are now believed to be based in Lebanon.[8]

In addition to housing Hamas leaders, Qatar provided Sheikh Al Qaradawi, a proponent of the Muslim Brotherhood and head of the International Union of Muslim Scholars, with air time on Al Jazeera.[9] During his show, Sheikh Al Qaradawi legitimized suicide bombings against Israelis, inspiring many of

---

[4] "Remarks of Under Secretary of Terrorism and Financial Intelligence David Cohen before the Center for a New American Security on 'Confronting New Threats in Terrorist Financing,'" U.S. Department of the Treasury, March 4, 2014, https://www.treasury.gov/press-center/press-releases/Pages/jl2308.aspx.

[5] Declan Walsh, "Hamas Leader Plays Final Hand: Trying to Lift Group's Pariah Status," *New York Times*, May 2, 2017, https://www.nytimes.com/2017/05/02/world/middleeast/hamas-khaled-meshal-gaza.html.

[6] Adnan Abu Amer, "Hamas Could Be Next Victim of Qatari-Gulf Brawl," Al-Monitor, June 8, 2017, http://www.al-monitor.com/pulse/en/originals/2017/06/hamas-leave-qatar-crisis-palestine.html.

[7] Peter Kovessy, "Qatar FM: Hamas Leader to Remain in Doha as 'Dear Guest,' *Doha News*, January 13, 2015, https://dohanews.co/qatar-fm-hamas-leader-remain-doha-dear-guest/.

[8] For more on Arouri, see Matthew Levitt, "Hamas' Not-so-Secret Weapon," *Foreign Affairs*, June 9, 2004, http://www.washingtoninstitute.org/policy-analysis/view/hamass-not-so-secret-weapon

[9] Walsh, "Qatar Opens Its Doors to All," https://www.nytimes.com/2017/07/16/world/middleeast/doha-qatar-blockade.html.

the attacks during the Second Intifada.[10] Though the Sheikh later retracted his statement and stopped his show in 2014, he remains a controversial Islamist leader who was given a platform at the hands of Qatar. His name is included in the recent list of 59 people that the blockading countries hope Qatar will deport and hold responsible for inciting terrorism.[11] While not designated himself, Qaradawi heads the Union of Good which is a US-designated umbrella charity group specifically created by Hamas leadership in late 2000 as a means of brokering the transfer of funds raised for Hamas around the world to the terrorist group in the West Bank and Gaza Strip. According to the U.S. Treasury Department, the Union of Good's executive leadership and board of directors includes Hamas leaders, Specially Designated Global Terrorists (SDGTs), and other terrorist supporters."[12]

Qatar has also hosted many leaders of the Afghan Taliban and became the group's center for diplomacy since the movement established an office in Doha in 2013.[13] That year, it was reported that more than 20 high-raking Taliban members and their families resided in Qatar.[14] In October 2016, Doha hosted meetings between the Taliban and representatives from the Afghani government. Mullah Abdul Manan Akhund, brother of the former Taliban chief Mullah Omar, was present at the meetings.

Qatar sees its ties to groups like Hamas and the Taliban as part of its legitimate foreign policy efforts, and notes that in both cases Western countries have taken advantage of its relationship to such groups for purposes such as furthering Afghan diplomatic efforts or other efforts such as funding for the Gaza Strip. And while that may be the case, it does not excuse harboring extremists involved in acts of terrorism and other political violence. It is a fact that Doha has become the preferred safe haven for a wide array of Islamist extremists beyond what foreign policy needs could possibly excuse.

Harboring Terrorist Financiers

In addition to hosting leaders of terrorist organizations, Qatar has been complacent in permitting terrorist financing within and outside of its border, despite signing agreements to curb such activity. While Qatar has made previous efforts to halt terrorist financing, the efficacy and sincerity of these efforts are questionable. In 2014, the State Department's Country Reports credited Qatar with shutting down Saad al-Kaabi's online fundraising platform for al Qaeda in Syria, Madad Ahl al-Sham.[15] However, in 2015, the U.S. Treasury designated al-Kaabi as a financial supporter of al-Qaeda and al-Qaeda's Syrian affiliate, Al-Nusrah Front (ANF).[16] Al-Kaabi was found responsible for raising funds for ANF to purchase weapons and food, as well facilitating the ransom payment for a hostage held by ANF in early 2014. Al-Kaabi worked for ANF in Syria since at least late 2012.[17] Al-Kaabi came up again in the context of the 2017 designation of a Kuwait-based terror financier, Mohammad al-Anizi, when Treasury noted that "in late 2015, al-Anizi sought assistance from AQ financier and U.S.- and U.N.-designated Sa'd al-Ka'bi to

---

[10] "The Cleric Who Legitimized Suicide Attacks against Israel Has Reversed His Ruling. Hamas Isn't Listening," *Times of Israel*, January 10, 2017, http://www.timesofisrael.com/the-cleric-who-legitimized-suicide-attacks-against-israel-has-reversed-his-ruling-hamas-isnt-listening/.

[11] Walsh, "Qatar Opens Its Doors to All," https://www.nytimes.com/2017/07/16/world/middleeast/doha-qatar-blockade.html.

[12] https://www.treasury.gov/resource-center/terrorist-illicit-finance/Pages/protecting-union-of-good.aspx.

[13] "Taliban and Afghanistan Restart Secret Talks in Qatar," *Guardian*, October 18, 2016, https://www.theguardian.com/world/2016/oct/18/taliban-afghanistan-secret-talks-qatar.

[14] "How Qatar Came to Host the Taliban," BBC News, June 22, 2013, http://www.bbc.com/news/world-asia-23007401.

[15] "Country Reports: Middle East and North Africa Overview," U.S. Department of State, 2014, https://www.state.gov/j/ct/rls/crt/2014/239407.htm.

[16] "Treasury Designates Financial Supporters of Al-Qaida and Al-Nusrah Front," U.S. Department of the Treasury, August 5, 2015, https://www.treasury.gov/press-center/press-releases/Pages/jl0143.aspx.

[17] Ibid.

facilitate the travel of AQ-associated individuals."[18] Evidently, al-Kaabi continued to provide funding for ANF even after Qatar supposedly shut down his fundraising platform in 2014, putting a large question mark over the integrity of Qatar's measures to stop terrorist financing.

In another case, the U.S. Treasury sanctioned 'Abd al-Malik 'Abd al-Salam (aka Umar al-Qatari), a Jordanian with Qatari residence.[19] In 2011 and 2012, he worked with associates in Turkey, Syria, Lebanon, Qatar, and Iran to raise and move funds, weapons, and facilitate travel for fighters. For example, in 2012, Umar al-Qatari gave thousands of dollars and material support to an al-Qaeda associate in Syria, intended to assist ANF operatives. That same year, he also assisted with ANF recruitment in Turkey. He has used online sites to raise funds for al-Qaida and in 2011 he was part of an attack against U.S. forces in Afghanistan.[20] In 2014, the State Department's Country Reports on Qatar said that the Qatari government had deported a Jordanian terrorist financier living in Doha and employed by a Qatari charity.[21] The report did not name the Jordanian deported, however, it is possible that they were referring to Umar al-Qatari. If it was in fact him, it is possible he continued to engage in terrorist financing for at least two years after he was designated by Treasury.

Doha has been particularly sketchy on the issue of the prosecution of terrorism financiers in Qatari courts. According to the State Department's 2015 Country Reports, Doha had "made efforts to prosecute significant terrorist financiers."[22] As of 2016, Qatar had prosecuted five terrorist financiers: Ibrahim al-Bakr,[23] Saad al-Kaabi,[24] Abd al-Latif al Kawari,[25] Abd al-Rahman al-Nuaymi,[26] and Khalifa al-Subaiey.[27] It is now clear that of these, two were acquitted, one was convicted but then acquitted on appeal, and one was convicted in absentia. As a result, none were in jail when the current intra-Gulf spat broke out, though the ones still resident in Qatar were reportedly under surveillance. According to recent reports, some new arrests have been made since the current crisis began, likely involving some of those previously tried in Qatari courts.

Despite shutting down al-Kaabi's fundraising platform in 2014, Qatar acquitted al-Kaabi in 2016, along with Abd al-Rahman al-Nuaymi.[28] Both were designated by the Treasury for providing support to al-Qaeda.[29] According to his Treasury designation, Nu'aymi ordered the transfer of almost $600,000 to al-

---

[18] "Treasury Sanctions Prominent Al-Nusrah Front and Al-Qa'ida Facilitator," U.S. Department of the Treasury, March 14, 2017, https://www.treasury.gov/press-center/press-releases/Pages/sm0027.aspx

[19] "Treasury Designates Twelve Foreign Terrorist Fighter Facilitators," U.S. Department of the Treasury, https://www.treasury.gov/press-center/press-releases/Pages/jl2651.aspx.

[20] Ibid.

[21] "Country Reports: Middle East and North Africa Overview," U.S. Department of State, 2014, https://www.state.gov/j/ct/rls/crt/2014/239407.htm.

[22] "Country Reports: Middle East and North Africa Overview," U.S. Department of State, 2015, https://www.state.gov/j/ct/rls/crt/2015/257517.htm.

[23] "Treasury Designates Twelve Foreign Terrorist Fighter Facilitators," U.S. Department of the Treasury, September 24, 2014. https://www.treasury.gov/press-center/press-releases/Pages/jl2651.aspx.

[24] "Treasury Designates Financial Supporters of Al-Qaida and Al-Nusrah Front," U.S. Department of the Treasury, August 5, 2015, https://www.treasury.gov/press-center/press-releases/Pages/jl0143.aspx.

[25] Ibid.

[26] "Treasury Designates Al-Qa'ida Supporters in Qatar and Yemen," U.S. Department of the Treasury, December 18, 2013. https://www.treasury.gov/press-center/press-releases/Pages/jl2249.aspx.

[27] "Treasury Designates Gulf-Based al Qaida Financiers," U.S. Department of the Treasury, June 5, 2008, https://www.treasury.gov/press-center/press-releases/Pages/hp1011.aspx.

[28] "Counter Terrorism Designations," U.S. Department of the Treasury, August 5, 2015, https://www.treasury.gov/resource-center/sanctions/OFAC-Enforcement/Pages/20150805.aspx.

[29] "Treasury Designates Al-Qa'ida Supporters in Qatar and Yemen," U.S. Department of the Treasury, December 18, 2013. https://www.treasury.gov/press-center/press-releases/Pages/jl2249.aspx.

Qaeda through an al-Qaeda representative in Syria. He also assisted with the financing of al-Qaeda in Iraq and was the middle-man between Qatari-based donors and al-Qaeda in Iraq.[30]

The three other individuals that Qatar prosecuted include Bakr, Kawari, and Subaiey. Bakr and Kawari were convicted in 2016 and Subaiey was convicted in 2008. This was the second time that Bakr was convicted, following his 2000 arrest in which he was subsequently "released from prison after he promised not to conduct terrorist activity in Qatar."[31] In his latest conviction, he was convicted in absentia and remains at large outside of Qatar. According to the 2008 Treasury designation, in 2006, Bakr assisted a terrorist cell that was plotting attacks against U.S. military bases in Qatar. Additionally, beginning in 2012, Bakr worked for al-Qaeda, serving as the link between Gulf-based al-Qaeda financiers and Afghanistan.[32]

Abd al-Latif al-Kawari, arrested in 2016 in Qatar and supposedly serving his sentence under house arrest, was designated in 2015 by the U.S. Treasury for coordinating the funding between Qatari funders and al-Qaeda. He also served as an al-Qaeda security official.[33]

Lastly, Khalifa al-Subaiey was originally arrested in January of 2008 in Bahrain for his "financing terrorism, undergoing terrorist training, facilitating the travel of others abroad to receive terrorist training, and for membership in a terrorist organization."[34] He was arrested again in March of 2008 by Qatar and served a six-month term in prison. He is supposedly under surveillance; however, in 2015 the UN Committee on al-Qaeda sanctions updated his listing with new information—which is no small matter because it required a new vote of the full UNSC—and reported that al-Subaiey had resumed terrorist activity. According to the Committee, "after his release, Al-Subaiey reconnected with Al-Qaida financiers and facilitators in the Middle East and resumed organizing funds in support of Al-Qaida. His involvement with Iran based facilitators continued in 2009, 2011 and throughout 2012 with money flowing to Al-Qaida leaders in Pakistan."[35] If he is in fact under Qatari surveillance, the Qatari authorities do not appear to be very vigilant.

Despite Qatar's half-hearted efforts to prosecute terrorist financiers, there are many others who Qatar has failed to prosecute or designate as terrorists. Eleven of the names from the U.S. lists also appear on the list of the Arab Quartet, and six of them overlap with the UN lists. Qatari officials maintain there are other cases of terror financiers—both Qataris and non-Qataris—who are resident in the country and are the subject of investigations with an eye toward prosecuting them.

It is important to note here that while terror finance prosecutions are difficult cases, and acquittals are part of a normally functioning justice system, these are not the only tools available to Qatari officials to deal with the terror financiers effectively serving as regional bundlers of terror funding from donors throughout the region to al Qaeda in Syria in particular. The first big test for Qatar will be to populate the domestic designated list created by the Emir's recent update to the country's 2004 counterterrorism law.

Qatari Counterterrorism Legislation and Agreements

---

[30] Ibid.

[31] "Treasury Designates Twelve Foreign Terrorist Fighter Facilitators," U.S. Department of the Treasury, September 24, 2014. https://www.treasury.gov/press-center/press-releases/Pages/jl2651.aspx.

[32] Ibid.

[33] "Treasury Designates Financial Supporters of Al-Qaida and Al-Nusrah Front," U.S. Department of the Treasury, August 5, 2015, https://www.treasury.gov/press-center/press-releases/Pages/jl0143.aspx.

[34] "Treasury Designates Gulf-Based al Qaida Financiers," U.S. Department of the Treasury, June 5, 2008, https://www.treasury.gov/press-center/press-releases/Pages/hp1011.aspx.

[35] "Narrative Summaries of Reasons for Listing," United Nations, February 19, 2015, https://www.un.org/sc/suborg/en/sanctions/1267/aq_sanctions_list/summaries/individual/khalifa-muhammad-turki-al-subaiy.

During Secretary of State Rex Tillerson's visit to the Gulf this past month, Qatari Foreign Minister Sheikh Mohammed bin Abdulrahman signed a memorandum of understanding (MOU) on countering terrorist financing.[36] The memorandum outlines a number of steps that the U.S. and Qatari governments will each take in the coming months and years to further dismantle terrorist financing networks and address global terrorist activities more broadly. As part of the agreement, U.S. officials will be posted at the Qatari prosecutor's office.[37]

In addition to the recent MOU, the Emir Sheikh Tamim bin Hamad al-Thani issued a royal decree amending Qatar's anti-terrorism laws last Thursday.[38] The decree, which amends a 2004 anti-terrorism law, provides definitions of terrorism, acts of terrorism, freezing funding, and terrorist financing. Furthermore, the amendments create two national terrorism lists and establish rules for placing individuals and groups on each list.[39]

What is not clear, however, is what these lists will be used for, what the difference is between these two lists, what the criteria are for getting on or off the lists, or if any names have been put on these inaugural lists. While the UAE Minister of State for Foreign Affairs Dr. Anwar Gargash has called the legislation "a step in the right direction,"[40] Qatar, however, has a history of failing to follow through on its counterterrorism legislation. Passing the law is not sufficient—the laws must be fully and effectively implemented. A look at the 2004 law here is instructive.

In 2004, Qatar passed a law criminalizing terror financing, established a Financial Intelligence Unit (FIU), and founded the Qatari Authority for Charitable Activities (QACA).[41] The Law on Combatting Terrorism gave the state the authority to prosecute individuals involved in terrorist activities, including providing material support, training and financing extremist groups. The FIU had a number of authorities, including the authority to receive "suspicious transaction reports related to money laundering and terrorism financing directly from all concerned entities in Qatar" and analyze "suspicious transaction reports and taking appropriate decisions thereon."[42] The QACA was responsible specifically for screening financial transactions made by Qatari charities to certify that such donations and transactions were solely intended for humanitarian causes and not covertly funding terrorist activities.[43]

Despite the 2004 legislative efforts, there was little follow through after the laws were implemented. According to the 2008 International Monetary Fund's (IMF) Country Reports on Qatar, one of the six factors that contributed to the failure of the FIU included its failure to "regularly review its own effectiveness in combating terrorist financing and money laundering."[44] Additionally, the administrative order creating the FIU was inconsistent with Qatar's anti-money laundering law.

---

[36] "U.S. to Deploy Officials in Qatar in Counterterrorism Accord—Source," Reuters, July 20, 2017, http://uk.reuters.com/article/uk-gulf-qatar-usa-idUKKBN1A51ZJ.

[37] Ibid.

[38] "Qatari Emir Amends Laws to Bolster Fight against Terrorism: Agency," Reuters, July 20, 2017, http://www.reuters.com/article/us-gulf-qatar-emir-idUSKBN1A52VY.

[39] Ibid.

[40] "UAE Hopes Pressure Bears Fruit after Qatar Changes Terror Laws," *National*, July 21, 2017, https://www.thenational.ae/world/uae-hopes-pressure-bears-fruit-after-qatar-changes-terror-laws-1.612917.

[41] "Qatar: Detailed Assessment Report on Anti–Money Laundering and Combating the Financing of Terrorism," International Monetary Fund, October 2008, https://www.imf.org/en/Publications/CR/Issues/2016/12/31/Qatar-Detailed-Assessment-Report-on-Anti-Money-Laundering-and-Combating-the-Financing-of-22396.

[42] Ibid.

[43] Ibid.

[44] Ibid.

Another law, passed in 2006, expanded charitable oversight and gave additional authorities to the Ministry of Civil Service and Housing Affairs.[45] This was a step in the right direction, however, when a Financial Action Task Force (FATF) mutual evaluation team came to inspect Qatar's anti-money laundering and counter-terror finance (AML/CFT) regime two years later, it found significant problems. The IMF reported that Qatar criminalized terrorist financing, "but in a very limited way."[46] The IMF assessed Qatar's system requiring the disclosure of currency transported across the border as "neither implemented nor effective."[47] And despite having authority to confiscate, freeze or seize funds tied to money laundering or terror finance, not a single confiscation had been ordered because not a single money laundering charge had been brought before the courts. To the contrary: The IMF reported that it appeared that "on one occasion, the [Qatari] authorities offered safe harbor to a person designated under [United Nations terrorism designation list] UNSCR 1267. No actions were taken with respect to this person's funds or other assets."[48]

In a surreal encounter in 2009, I experienced firsthand Qatar's penchant for passing legislation and considering the matter closed without any implementation or enforcement. In a meeting with Qatari officials in Doha, I asked how the Qatari FIU assessed the compliance of local Hawalas (informal money transfer businesses common in the region) with a then-new law requiring Hawalas to register with the government or shut down. The official explained—with a straight face—that there appeared to be no Hawalas operating in the country since none had registered with the authorities as required under the new law. In fact, the official had an identical conversation with IMF assessors just a few weeks earlier. Highly skeptical that not a single Hawala operated in the country, IMF experts returned to their hotels and asked expatriate foreign workers how they sent money back to their families in their home countries. Their answers were hardly surprising: "Hawalas." The IMF team returned to the official with a long list of Hawalas operating openly in Qatar, required the government submit an updated section of its report on this issue to the IMF, and stressed the need to actually implement and enforce new laws.

In 2010, Qatar passed the Combatting Money Laundering and Terrorist Finance Law which specifically required prosecutors to freeze funds of UN-designated terrorist organizations.[49] The law outlined penalties for terrorist financing and money laundering, including penalties and fines. Despite this positive step towards AML/CTF and transparency, the law left the terms, conditions, and time limits of the freezing of funds up to the Public Prosecutor's discretion.[50] In practice, this law was not fully implemented in a timely manner. According to the State Department's 2012 Country Reports on Terrorism, "the government has begun to distribute lists of UN-designated terrorist entities and individuals to financial institutions. Implementation, however, remained inconsistent."[51]

Up until last week, Qatar's most recent CT legislation was passed in September 2014. The Law Regulating Charitable Activities, based on FATF standards, created the Charities Commission as an independent, interagency government board aiming to counter-terrorist financing by monitoring

---

[45] "Country Reports: Middle East and North Africa Overview." U.S. Department of State, 2014, https://www.state.gov/j/ct/rls/crt/2014/239407.htm.

[46] "Qatar: Detailed Assessment Report on Anti-Money Laundering," https://www.imf.org/en/Publications/CR/Issues/2016/12/31/Qatar-Detailed-Assessment-Report-on-Anti-Money-Laundering-and-Combating-the-Financing-of-22396.

[47] Ibid.

[48] Ibid.

[49] "Combatting Money Laundering and Terrorism Financing," Qatar Financial Centre Regulatory Authority," 2010, http://www.qfcra.com/en-us/legislation/Laws/Anti-Money Laundering Law No. (4) of 2010.pdf.

[50] Ibid.

[51] "Country Reports on Terrorism 2012," U.S. Department of State, 2012. https://www.state.gov/j/ct/rls/crt/2012/

transactions of charity organizations.[52] This law was ready in draft form in 2013, but was only passed in 2014 under significant international pressure. In 2013, the State Department noted that "formally" the Qatari Ministry of Labor and Social Affairs monitors and licenses nongovernmental charitable organizations and requires their foreign partners to submit to a vetting and licensing process.[53] In fact, this has not happened, in part because so long as charities operated within the Qatar Financial Center (QFC), they were exempt from having to register or be subject to supervision.

In September 2014, Qatar also signed on to the Jeddah Communique, a U.S.-led agreement in which Qatar, in addition to several other Gulf States, pledged to "end impunity and bring perpetrators to justice" and "repudiate hateful ideology."[54]

Despite the above legislative efforts, according to former senior U.S. Treasury official Daniel Glaser, U.S.- and UN-designated terrorist financiers continue to operate "openly and notoriously" in Qatar.[55] In February 2017, Glaser lamented that Qatar had not yet made the kind of "fundamental decisions" on combating terror finance that would make the country a hostile environment for terror financiers, concluding that the positive steps Qatar had taken were "painfully slow."[56]

In the just-released 2016 edition, the State Department noted that "Qatar has made significant progress on deficiencies identified in its MENAFATF Mutual Evaluation Report in 2008," adding that "According to the Second Biennial Update Report, Qatar is deemed 'Compliant or Largely Compliant' with all but recommendation 26, which accounts for regulation and supervision of financial institutions."[57] Regulation of Qatar's formal financial system is only part of the issue, however. As of the State Department's 2015 International Narcotics Control and Strategy Report, Qatar was at that time still listed as a country of primary concern. One reason, the department noted, was that "exploitation of charities to finance terrorism continues to be a concern, as does the ability of individuals to bypass the formal financial sector for illicit financing."[58] Moreover, that is not the only area demanding significantly more effort on the part of Doha to get up to speed on efforts to counter terror financing within the country.

Moving Forward

The recent MOU and amendments are important steps to ensuring Qatar seriously addresses the ongoing issue of terrorist financing happening within and beyond its borders. However, Doha has a weak track record of implementing and enforcing the terms of agreements. Moreover, the steps they have taken thus far are vague, and it is unclear to what extent they will actually address the ongoing issues in Qatar.

There are other concrete steps that Qatar may take in the coming months. In early June, Saudi Arabia, the United Arab Emirates, Egypt and Bahrain collectively designated 59 individuals and 12 institutions

---

[52] "Country Reports on Terrorism 2016," U.S. Department of State, July 2017, https://www.state.gov/documents/organization/272488.pdf.

[53] "Country Reports: Middle East and North Africa Overview," U.S. Department of State, 2013, https://www.state.gov/j/ct/rls/crt/2013/224823.htm.

[54] "Country Reports: Middle East and North Africa Overview," U.S. Department of State, 2014, https://www.state.gov/j/ct/rls/crt/2014/239407.htm.

[55] Daniel Glaser. Foundation for Defense of Democracies, February 7, 2017, https://www.youtube.com/watch?v=OXSMKYr-SFI&feature=youtu.be&t=34m18s.

[56] Ibid.

[57] "Country Reports: Qatar," U.S. Department of State, 2016, https://www.state.gov/documents/organization/272488.pdf.

[58] "Countries/Jurisdictions of Primary Concern-Qatar," 2015 International Narcotics Control Strategy Report (INCSR), U.S. Department of State, https://www.state.gov/j/inl/rls/nrcrpt/2015/supplemental/239287.htm.

accused of financing terrorist organizations and receiving support from Qatar.[59] Many of these entities were previously designated by the United States and United Nations for financing al-Qaeda, though the list includes others with ties to Muslim Brotherhood and Salafi extremists in Egypt, Libya, and elsewhere. Some of those listed are not Qatar residents, and according to a Qatari official, at least six of the people listed are dead.

The list provides Doha an opportunity to help resolve its fight with its Gulf Cooperation Council neighbors, and a way to save face while doing so. It could immediately take action at least against those persons and entities on the list that are already designated by the U.S. or U.N. and therefore should already have been targeted by Doha. In particular, Qatar could focus on the many al-Qaeda financiers on the list, and take action based on their recent (re)commitment to counter terrorist finance at the recent Riyadh summit and in the MOU just signed with the United States.

Qatar must take the opportunity to change behaviors that have been tolerated for far too long, but the coalition of four countries that have broken diplomatic and trade relations with Qatar must be flexible enough to allow Doha to do so in a manner that saves face for all parties involved. Most importantly, whatever laws are enacted or agreements entered into must be fully implemented and enforced. Actions taken in the name of countering terrorism must be substantive and verifiable, which would be a welcome change from past patterns of behavior.

---

[59] "43 New Designations Specifically Address Threats Posed by Qatar Linked and Based Al Qaida Terrorism Support Networks," Emirates News Agency, July 24, 2017, http://wam.ae/en/details/1395302618259.

Mrs. WAGNER. Thank you, Dr. Levitt, for your testimony.
I now turn to Mr. Goldenberg for your opening statement.

STATEMENT OF MR. ILAN GOLDENBERG, SENIOR FELLOW AND DIRECTOR, MIDDLE EAST SECURITY PROGRAM, CENTER FOR A NEW AMERICAN SECURITY

Mr. GOLDENBERG. Madam Chairman, Ranking Member Deutch, distinguished members of the subcommittee, thank you for the opportunity to testify today on the U.S.-Qatar relationship and the implications of the current divisions within the Gulf Cooperation Council. My objective with this testimony is not to recount the various moves and countermoves each side has made in the past few weeks since the crisis erupted. Instead, I will provide some context as to what created this situation, the implications for U.S. interests, and the possible way ahead.

Qatar is a complex American partner, to say the least. On the one hand, it has pursued a policy that has included building relations with a number of actors the United States finds problematic, including extremist groups in Syria, the Taliban, Hamas, and the Muslim Brotherhood. This approach has been part of an independent, and sometimes provocative Qatari foreign policy that has chaffed on some of its Gulf neighbors and, in some instances, these neighbors have viewed Qatari reactions as interfering in their own internal affairs, which infuriated them and been a major reason for the recent actions.

From an American perspective, the Qatari policy in Syria and the slow response to terror financing were probably most problematic. When the Syrian civil war erupted, Qatar was on the forefront in providing financial aid and weaponry to the Syrian opposition groups of all stripes with little control or oversight. The Qataris were far from alone in committing this mistake as a number of other Gulf state-actors, as well as Turkey also pursued an anybody-but-Assad policy without fully vetting some of these anybodies.

Certainly, the United States made its own share of mistakes during this time period. While Qatar and Turkey in particular were the most aggressive in funding some of the more ideologically extremist groups, including al-Qaeda affiliate, Jebhat al-Nusra, and we are still living with these mistakes in Syria and will be for years to come.

But on some issues, Qatar has been a useful partner. Qatar hosts a critical U.S. air base with more than 10,000 American troops. Al Udeid Air Base is a central node from which the United States conducts air operations in Iraq, Syria, and Afghanistan, as well as other operations across the Middle East.

The bases hosted U.S. military aircraft for over 15 years, and during that time, has been a reliable partner, allowing access for a broad array of military operations.

Moreover, Qatar's flexible approach to problematic actors has, at times, made it a useful connector when the diplomacy inevitably requires negotiation and engagement with unsavory characters.

Take for example, Qatar's relationship with Hamas and the aid it provides in Gaza. On the one hand, both the United States and Israel designated Hamas as a terrorist organization. On the other, Israel has cooperated quietly with Qatar in recent years to ensure financial assistance gets into Gaza in order to try to improve the situation on the ground and avoid another conflict. Whether one chooses to view Qatar positively or negatively, what is clear is that the inter-GCC split that has emerged in recent weeks has not been good for U.S. interests. Only 2 weeks after President Trump visited Riyadh to unify the Arab world behind the common objectives of countering extremism and pushing back on Iran, America's Gulf allies have launched into an internal feud that has largely distracted them and us.

Meanwhile, the split has created new opportunities for Russia and Iran to increase their influence in the region. Going forward, the Trump administration should take a number of steps.

First, settle on one consistent message and approach instead of open breaks between the President and the Secretary of State, which only cause confusion and undermine our ability to mediate in this crisis.

Second, move away from viewing the Middle East through a pure black and white prism. The Trump administration focused so heavily on unifying and backing the Sunni, Arab states, they fail to recognize the internal splits among them. This inadvertently gave a green light to some of our Gulf partners to move ahead with these actions against Qatar.

Third, settle in for the long haul, as this crisis is not going to be solved any time soon. We should clearly signal to our partners that we are still focused on the challenges posed by ISIS and Iran, and we expect them to do the same instead of focusing all their diplomatic energy on trying to convince Washington to take their side in this fight.

Fourth, encourage de-escalation on all sides by at least getting them all to tone down their public rhetoric while emphasizing that the U.S. is willing to play a constructive mediating role.

However, it is ultimately an inter-Arab disagreement that they will need to be out in front in solving.

And, finally, fifth, I think we should use this crisis as an opportunity to engage with all the countries of the GCC to shine more of a light on the problem of terror financing. As some of the other witnesses and members have said, Qatar certainly is a major problematic actor in this space, but it is far from the only one, and this could actually be an opportunity, in terms of this crisis, to actually push all of them to be better on this issue.

So thank you very much, and I look forward to answering your questions.

[The prepared statement of Mr. Goldenberg follows:]

Center for a
New American
Security

July 26, 2017

Testimony before the House Foreign Affairs Committee – Subcommittee on the Middle East and North Africa

Assessing the U.S.-Qatar Relationship

Ilan Goldenberg, Senior Fellow and Director, Middle East Security Program
Center for a New American Security

Chairman Ros-Lehtinen, Ranking Member Deutch, distinguished members of the committee, thank you for the opportunity to testify today on the U.S-Qatar relationship and the implications of the current divisions within the Gulf Cooperation Council (GCC).[1]

On June 4, 2017, Saudi Arabia, the United Arab Emirates, Bahrain, and Egypt announced they would cut ties with Qatar and take a number of steps against it; including cutting off access to airspace and borders and ejecting Qatari diplomats and citizens from these countries. Since then, the war of words has escalated on all sides. The United States has tried to play a role as a mediator, but thus far with little success. My objective with this testimony is not to recount the various moves and counter moves each side has made in the past few weeks, but instead to provide some context as to what created this situation, the implications for U.S. interests, and the potential way ahead.

Qatar is a complex American partner. On one hand, it has pursued a policy that has included building relations with a number of actors that the United States finds highly problematic, including extremist groups in Syria, the Taliban, Hamas, and the Muslim Brotherhood. On the other, it is host to a critical U.S. airbase and its flexible approach to these actors has made it a useful connector when diplomacy inevitably requires negotiation and engagement with unsavory characters.

---

[1] CNAS accepted contributions from the Embassy of the United Arab Emirates in fiscal years 2016 and 2017 for the total amount of $250,000 in support of a project evaluating the pros and cons of the United Arab Emirates' seeking membership in the Missile Technology Control Regime (MTCR). CNAS produced a briefing for the UAE Embassy on the MTCR. The background research on the MTCR also informed an already ongoing CNAS project on drone proliferation policy. The public report can be found at http://drones.cnas.org/reports/drone-proliferation/. CNAS is a national security research and policy institution committed to the highest standards of organizational, intellectual, and personal integrity. The Center retains sole editorial control over its ideas, projects, and productions, and the content of its publications reflects only the views of their authors. In keeping with its mission and values, CNAS does not engage in lobbying activity and complies fully with all applicable federal, state, and local laws. Accordingly, CNAS will not engage in any representation or advocacy on behalf of any entities or interests and, to the extent that the Center accepts funding from foreign sources, its activities will be limited to bona fide scholastic, academic, and research-related activities, consistent with applicable federal law. A full list of CNAS supporters and the center's funding guidelines can be found here: https://www.cnas.org/support-cnas

But whether one chooses to view Qatar positively or negatively, it is clear is that the intra-GCC split that has emerged in recent weeks has not been good for U.S. interests. Only two weeks after President Trump visited Riyadh to unify the Arab world behind the common objectives of countering extremism and pushing back on Iran, America's Gulf allies have launched an internal feud that has largely distracted them and the United States. Meanwhile, this split has created new opportunities for Russia and Iran.

Going forward, the Trump administration should take a number of steps. First, it should settle on one consistent message and approach, as conflicting messages from the President and Secretary of State cause confusion and undermine the United States' ability to mediate. Second, it should move away from viewing the Middle East through a purely black and white prism, as this approach focused so heavily on unifying and backing the Sunni Arab states that it failed to recognize the internal splits among them and inadvertently gave a green light to some U.S. Gulf partners to move ahead with these actions against Qatar. Third, as this crisis is not going to be solved anytime soon, the administration should settle in for the long haul and push all of the actors to start putting more of their energies back into the ISIS and Iran challenges. And fourth, it should encourage deescalation on all sides by at least getting U.S. partners to tone down their public rhetoric and maximalist public ultimatums and emphasize that while the U.S. is willing to play a constructive mediating role this is ultimately an intra-Arab disagreement that they will need to be at the forefront of solving.

Sources of Disagreement Between Qatar and Its GCC Neighbors

Qatar is far from an ideal partner and a number of its actions over the years have frustrated many of its Gulf neighbors as well as the United States. Indeed, Qatar has long been the black sheep of the Gulf Cooperation Council due to the independent foreign policy that it has pursued for the past twenty years – often in direct competition with Saudi Arabia and other GCC neighbors.

One of the most significant disagreements between Qatar and its neighbors has been over differing perspectives on the Muslim Brotherhood. With the start of protests across the Arab world in 2011, the Qataris supported Muslim Brotherhood–affiliated movements, while the Emiratis and Saudis viewed them as a major threat to regional stability. In Egypt, Qatar supported the then-elected Muslim Brotherhood government of Mohammed Morsi, providing his government with $8 billion during its one year in office.[2] Meanwhile, the other Gulf states supported Gen. Abdel-Fattah el-Sissi, who overthrew the Brotherhood and initiated a broad crackdown against it. They infused $23 billion of aid into Egypt in the 18 months after the Brotherhood was overthrown.[3]

Qatar's support for Islamist groups also extends to Hamas. Qatar has hosted Hamas's political leadership in Doha since 2012 and been a major contributor of aid into Gaza – a fair amount of which gets diverted by Hamas for nefarious purposes. And the disagreement over Islamists has also

---

[2] Robert F. Worth, "Egypt Is Arena for Influence of Arab Rivals." *The New York Times*, July 9, 2013. http://www.nytimes.com/2013/07/10/world/middleeast/aid-to-egypt-from-saudis-and-emiratis-is-part-of-struggle-with-qatar-for-influence.html.
[3] Andrew Torchia, "Egypt Got $23 Billion in Aid from Gulf in 18 Months: Minister." *Reuters*, March 2, 2015. http://www.reuters.com/article/us-egypt-investment-gulf-idUSKBN0LY0V620150302.

flowed into Qatari willingness to host Islamist dissidents that have been ejected from some of its regional partners. Additionally, Qatar's use of the Al Jazeera television station to attack Saudi Arabia and the UAE has infuriated Riyadh and Abu Dhabi.[4]

From an American perspective, Qatari policy in Syria and its slow response to terror financing are even more problematic. When the Syrian civil war erupted in 2011, Qatar was at the forefront of providing financial aid and weaponry — with little control or oversight — to Syrian opposition groups of all stripes. The Qataris were far from alone in committing this mistake, as a number of other Gulf state actors as well as Turkey pursued an "anybody but Assad" policy without fully vetting some of these "anybodies." Certainly the United States made its own share of mistakes during this time period. If it had taken on a more hands-on role in supporting the opposition, it may have been able to steer some of its partners to invest more wisely in groups more amenable to its interests. And even when the United States did engage more in supporting opposition groups, American weapons found their way into extremist hands.[5] But Qatar and Turkey in particular were the most aggressive in funding some of the more ideologically extremist groups including the al Qaeda affiliate Jebhat al Nusra. This caused a significant increase of Jihadist influence inside the Syrian opposition.[6] And more broadly beyond Syria, the Qataris have been slower than other Gulf states in taking steps to curb terror financing.[7] It is important to note, however, that other Gulf partners continue to exhibit problematic behavior.

Qatar and its neighbors have clashed over differing views on Iran. Saudi Arabia views Iran's Islamic Republic as an implacable enemy and the greatest threat in the Middle East. On the other hand, for practical economic reasons Qatar takes a more accommodationist approach to Iran. Qatar and Iran share the world's largest offshore gas field, which Doha calls the North Field and Iran calls South Pars. This field accounts for nearly all of Qatar's gas production and nearly 60 percent of its export revenue.[8] This does not mean that the Qataris have been completely sanguine about some of Iran's problematic regional behavior and support for various proxies in the Middle East. And the Qataris have not aligned with Iran. But they simply are not in a position to take as a hard of a line as some of their GCC partners. Though it is important to note that some other members of the GCC — most notably Oman — also pursue a strategy similar to Qatar's.

Qatar's Value as a U.S. Partner

Despite disagreements on some important issues, Qatar has been a valuable U.S. partner. Most importantly, Qatar's Al-Udeid Air Force base hosts more than 10,000 American troops and is a

---

[4] Kristian Coates Ulrichsen, "Qatar: The Gulf's Problem Child." *The Atlantic*, June 5, 2017. https://www.theatlantic.com/international/archive/2017/06/qatar-gcc-saudi-arabia-yemen-bahrain/529227/.

[5] Bradford Richardson, "US-Trained Syrian Rebels Gave Weapons to Al Qaeda, Pentagon Admits," *The Hill*, September 26, 2015. http://thehill.com/policy/defense/255055-us-trained-sytian-rebels-gave-weapons-to-al-qaeda-pentagon-admits.

[6] Liz Sly, and Zakaria Zakaria, "'Al-Qaeda Is Eating Us': Syrian Rebels Are Losing out to Extremists," *The Washington Post*, February 23, 2017. https://www.washingtonpost.com/world/middle_east/al-qaeda-is-eating-us-syrian-rebels-are-losing-out-to-extremists/2017/02/23/f9c6d1d4-f885-11e6-aa1e-5f735ee31334_story.html?utm_term=.40846df6e6f1.

[7] Matthew Levitt, and Katherine Bauer, "Qatar Doesn't Need a Blockade. It Needs an Audit." *Foreign Policy*, June 15, 2017. http://foreignpolicy.com/2017/06/15/qatar-doesnt-need-a-blockade-it-needs-an-audit-al-qaeda/.

[8] Tom Finn, "Qatar Restarts Development of World's Biggest Gas Field after 12-Year Freeze." *Reuters*, April 3, 2017. http://www.reuters.com/article/us-qatar-gas-idUSKBN175181.

central node from which the United States conducts air operations in Iraq, Syria, and Afghanistan as well as other operations across the Middle East.[9] It is the home of USCENTCOM's Combined Air Operation Center (CAOC) from which all American air operations are coordinated. And USCENTCOM's forward headquarters is also in Al Udeid — making it an important command and control hub in the event of a major military contingency in the Middle East. The base has hosted U.S. military aircraft for over 15 years and during that time has been a reliable partner, allowing access for a broad array of military operations.[10] This is one of the central reasons why Secretary Tillerson and Secretary Mattis have been so reluctant to take sides in the current intra-GCC dispute and have instead sought to mediate an end to the disagreement.

It is important to note that the base does not give Qatar absolute leverage over the United States, and indeed, the Qataris have traditionally refrained from trying to use the base as leverage or bringing it into broader political discussions. If the United States were to lose access, it would still have a number of major military bases in the Gulf and Central Asia that it could use to offset this loss. It could also seek to build new facilities in partner nations or, in the event of an emergency, rely on resources like an additional carrier strike group to offset these losses. But the reality is that these types of steps would be financially costly. They would also likely involve at least some reduction in U.S. capacity to conduct strikes against ISIS and in Afghanistan. And if the United States moved other naval assets into the region to compensate, those assets would have to come from elsewhere — most likely the Pacific. This would then hurt the U.S. ability to counter or deter China and North Korea. So, while the al-Udeid airbase is not an absolute necessity, losing it would come with a very real cost.

In addition to the importance of al-Udeid, Qatar has also sometimes played a useful role as a connector because of its willingness to host groups that the Untied States finds problematic. Take for example Qatar's relationships with Hamas and its role in Gaza. Even while Israeli officials continue to strongly oppose Qatar's relationship with Hamas, they acknowledge that the Qataris have played a constructive role in flowing aid to Gaza.[11] Because of intra-Palestinian politics, the Palestinian Authority and Fatah have taken a completely uncompromising position toward Hamas and have done all they can to squeeze Gaza. The Israeli government on the other hand has started to recognize that this policy leads to an unsustainable situation. There is a danger that if pressure in Gaza becomes too intense, the people turn on Hamas, creating political incentives for Hamas to provoke a conflict with Israel that allows it to regain political support but only at a great cost to all the parties involved. Israel has seen this cycle before and does not want to repeat it. Therefore, in recent years, Israel has looked the other way and in some cases worked quietly with the Qataris to ensure aid gets into Gaza, even recognizing that portions of it get diverted to support Hamas. If this Qatari aid were to evaporate the likelihood of another war in Gaza would increase.

---

[9] Tara Copp, "Pentagon: Al-Udeid Air Base Still Open, but US Prepared in Case Qatar Rift Escalates." *Military Times*, July 18, 2017. http://www.militarytimes.com/news/pentagon-congress/2017/07/17/pentagon-al-udeid-air-base-still-open-but-us-prepared-in-case-qatar-rift-escalates/.

[10] Greg Jaffe, and Thomas Gibbons-Neff, "For Qataris, a U.S. Air Base Is Best Defense against Trump Attacks." *The Washington Post*, June 6, 2017. https://www.washingtonpost.com/news/checkpoint/wp/2017/06/06/for-qataris-a-u-s-air-base-is-best-defense-against-trump-attacks/?utm_term=.475a80a48f81.

[11] Barbara Tasch, "Here's Why Israel Is Helping Qatar Aid Hamas in the Gaza Strip." *Business Insider*, June 18, 2015. http://www.businessinsider.com/why-israel-allows-qatar-to-support-hamas-in-gaza-2015-6.

Qatar has also come under criticism for allowing a permissive environment for Taliban representatives to operate in. But at the same time, it has hosted peace talks with the Taliban and often acted as a conduit for the United States in efforts to negotiate agreements to end the Afghan war.[12] From Libya, to Sudan, to Lebanon, Qatar's willingness to host various groups and take all sides has made Doha a useful location for holding peace talks and trying to reach agreements to end various regional conflicts.

Implications for the United States and the Way Ahead

Overall, from the American perspective the picture of Qatar is one of an imperfect partner. The United States has real and important disagreements with Qatar and would like to see its behavior on some issues change, but on other matters Qatar has been a valuable partner who has helped promote U.S. interests. In this context, the recent public split between Qatar and its neighbors has been damaging to U.S. interests, yet it is hard to see any resolution in the near future.

The most important consequence of the GCC split is that it has created a new massive distraction in the Middle East. In May, President Trump traveled to Saudi Arabia where he brought leaders from across the Arab World together to focus on two priorities: 1) fighting ISIS and other extremist groups; and 2) countering Iran. And yet two months later many of the United States' most important partners in this fight are dedicating the majority of their diplomatic efforts not to those objectives, but instead to countering each other and making the case in Washington for their positions. Meanwhile, even Secretary Tillerson has focused most of his diplomatic efforts in the Middle East on mediating an end to this conflict, which means he has less time dedicated to the challenges posed by ISIS and Iran.

The divides within the Arab world also give Russia and Iran more room to meddle in Arab politics and to insert themselves into regional affairs — as is evident from Moscow's assertive diplomacy with Doha and Tehran's offer to airlift food into Qatar to compensate for the Saudi blockade.[13] The intra-Arab split further reduces American influence. Indeed, numerous regional actors have already taken sides. Turkey has weighed in on Qatar's behalf and deployed forces to Qatar. Iraq has found itself awkwardly stuck in the middle. Iran has taken advantage of the division and aligned itself with Qatar in an attempt to draw it closer. And Moscow is clearly pleased to see this division among American partners.

Going forward, the Trump administration should take various steps to adjust its current policy and respond to this crisis. First, it needs to have one clear message to all of its partners. The President cannot publicly criticize Qatar while the Secretary of State simultaneously assumes the posture of an objective mediator. This simply undercuts any efforts at diplomacy, as all the players are confused about U.S. policy and choose to hear what is most in their interest. Indeed, the Saudis and Emiratis

---

12 Declan Walsh, "Qatar Opens Its Doors to All, to the Dismay of Some." *The New York Times*, July 16, 2017. https://www.nytimes.com/2017/07/16/world/middleeast/doha-qatar-blockade.html?_r=0.
13 "Russian, Qatari Foreign Ministers to Discuss Diplomatic Crisis in Middle East." *TASS*, June 10, 2017. http://tass.com/politics/950827.

primarily have tried to go through a more sympathetic White House, while the Qataris engage with the Pentagon and the State Department.

Second, the administration must stop viewing the Middle East through a simple black and white perspective. It was no coincidence that Saudi Arabia, the UAE, Egypt, and Bahrain decided to act against Qatar only weeks after the President's visit to Riyadh. These countries walked out of Riyadh believing that they had a blank check from the President and that he would support them no matter what. And while this crisis is not the Trump administration's fault and is ultimately about intra-Arab disagreements, this sense of impunity undoubtedly played a role in these states' decision to sever ties with Qatar.

Instead of a blank check, a better approach would be to offer Saudi Arabia a clear quid pro-quo: the United States will recognize Riyadh's leadership in the region and will do more to counter Iranian influence if the kingdom will do more get its own house in order by setting aside intra-Arab disputes, mitigating the fierce polarization (mostly over Islamism) within and between Arab societies, and focusing Arab efforts directly on Iran and the Islamic State – the threats both agree are top priorities.

Third, the United States should accept the reality that this split is going to be around for a while and start preparing to deal with it as a long-term, persistent problem instead of just a crisis to be solved. All parties have taken public and uncompromising positions, which means resolution anytime in the near future is unlikely. Instead of high-profile shuttle diplomacy, what is needed is quieter work behind the scenes and a resumed focus on other major challenges that the United States shares with its GCC partners.

The first message to U.S. partners needs to be that it is still focused on the challenges posed by ISIS and Iran and that the United States expects them to remain focused on those challenges as well. Even as the United States continues to manage this disagreement, its focus is returning to the bigger challenges the region faces. And it expects its partners to do the same instead of focusing their diplomatic energy on trying to convince Washington to take their side in this fight.

At the same time, the United States should emphasize to all sides that it expects them to deescalate the public rhetoric surrounding the disagreement and stop the media war. If the United States can persuade them to tone down the rhetoric and public stories, then over time there may be more political flexibility to reach an agreement. The United States should also make clear that it is willing to play a central role in any mediated outcome and essentially act as a guarantor of any agreement. However, it must recognize that this is ultimately an intra-Arab disagreement and they must take the lead in solving it.

Finally, the United States can use this crisis as an opportunity to engage with all of the GCC actors in trying to change behavior that it finds problematic. When it comes to terror financing, there is now an opportunity to create one level bar that the United States expects all its regional partners to abide by. Qatar may have been slower than some of the other GCC partners to address terror financing challenges, but the reality is that Saudi Arabia and Kuwait in particular still have huge challenges. The United States should use this crisis to press all of them to clean up their acts.

Mrs. WAGNER. Thank you, Mr. Goldenberg.

And I thank all of our witnesses for their opening statements.

I would like to open up my line of questioning by recognizing the fact that I think this hearing is very timely. Both Qatar and the Gulf countries have been important partners, and we would like to see a constructive, honest resolution to the crisis.

Qatar is a military ally of the United States, but has simultaneously supported Hamas and al-Qaeda. We have a role in easing tensions in the region, but not at the expense of our national security interests and our values. Qatar must cut ties with terrorists; our allies cannot provide support to our enemies.

Dr. Schanzer, I have no sympathy for supporters of Hamas, nor do you.

You have called the U.S. base in Qatar an "insane arrangement," I think is the quote. Do you believe the base location is dangerous? And how would you propose safely moving the base in such a way that doesn't compromise operations in the region?

Mr. SCHANZER. Congresswoman Wagner, thank you for the question. Look, I would probably put it this way: First of all, it is an insane arrangement. The idea that you have this forward air base that is conducting the most crucial operations in the war on terrorism, and that is it mere miles away from the Taliban presence, Hamas presence where there are designated terror financiers from the Nusra front running around in Doha. This sends the wrong message. It sends the wrong message to the United States and to our allies in the coalition to fight ISIS and al-Qaeda. It sends the wrong message to our Middle East allies as well.

In other words, when we tell them that we are going to hold them to account for their terror financing issues, and then they look at what is going on in Qatar, the optics, I think, are really rather terrible.

As for the safety of our troops, so far I would say, so good. We have not had incidents where it appears that our troops are being threatened. I would actually say that is not the case with Incirlik Air Base in Turkey, which is another country that supports some of these terror groups.

But at the end of the day, our recommendation has been that we begin to assess what it would take to move the base. Maybe not all of it. Maybe not all of it at once, but we need to take a look regionally at the other areas where we may be able to base some of these assets and to signal to the Qataris that we are willing to move. We don't need to do it. We may decide at the end of the day, the Pentagon may decide they can't afford to do it, it is too difficult, but in the meantime, it is important to message to the appropriate people in Qatar that we are willing to look at this problem and to reallocate assets as necessary.

Mrs. WAGNER. Thank you.

Dr. Levitt, can you discuss what actions the Saudis and other Gulf states have taken to combat terror financing that the Qataris have not?

Mr. LEVITT. Thank you for the question. You know, terror financing is a problem throughout the Gulf, and it took the Saudis some time to get on top of this problem.

For a long time, U.S. Treasury pointed to Saudi Arabia as the epicenter of this problem, but the Saudis turned a corner. There is more that they can do, but the Saudis now run intelligence operations. They prosecute people. They work with us in designating people. There have even been joint U.S.-Saudi designations including of charities and individuals in Saudi Arabia.

That is domestically difficult politically for them, but they have done it. There is more that they can do, but we now tend to point to others within the GCC toward Saudi Arabia, and we are trying to show them what we would like them—the types of things we would like to do more.

There is an irony that Kuwait is the country that is kind of playing the middleman on this, and Kuwait is often described as being just as bad as Qatar on terror finance. And that is something that we need to recognize as well. But the fact is that there are things that Qatar should have done a long time ago, and that they have not done, and that we have, frankly, tolerated them not doing. And the overt financing of effectively the most important al-Qaeda entity in the world, al-Qaeda and Saudi Arabia, is completely beyond the pale.

Mrs. WAGNER. Thank you.

Mr. Goldenberg, in my limited time here, one of the demands from the Gulf states was that Qatar must close down the Turkish military base. I get that they are concerned about the Muslim Brotherhood's influence. But how important do you think this demand is in terms of regional stability and security, and is this one that should be dropped?

Mr. GOLDENBERG. Thank you, Congresswoman, for the question.

I think that on the list of demands, the Turkish air base is probably lower—the base is lower on the list of demands that the Emiratis and the Saudis and others are leveling. In most conversations, what you hear them really focusing on is, more has to do with what the Qataris might be doing in the press, than some of the sort of the personal attacks at certain point that the different sides are launching at each other right now. I think that is much more the source of the issue, and the terror financing issue that we have been talking about has been much more central to the debate than this Turkish base, that, frankly, there have been already a move for the Turks to deploy some forces there a couple of years ago, and then when this crisis erupted, they moved everything up; they moved it very quickly to sort of a symbolic step. It is a good example of an opportunity, or the crisis, and the move has actually backfired on some of our partners, if what they were trying to do was isolate Qatar. What they actually managed to do is strengthen the Turkey-Qatar relationship instead.

So I would put this one probably as not as central as some of the other questions that have been out there before, but something that we will see as time goes on if they walk away from.

Mrs. WAGNER. Thank you for that insight. My time has elapsed.

I now recognize the ranking member, Mr. Deutch, for 5 minutes.

Mr. DEUTCH. Thank you, Madam Chairman.

Mr. Goldenberg, you referred to the flexible approach to problematic actors. And—so the question I have for you and for the panel is, how can—what is that? How is it—here is how it is characterized. Right? It is characterized as, well, yes, we know that Hamas is a terrorist organization, but if our ally has a relationship, then perhaps that can help us somehow.

Dr. Schanzer, I presume, would argue that Hamas is Hamas, and we should have nothing to do with them and our allies shouldn't either. Yet, the question is what does that flexible approach get us?

And, Dr. Schanzer, if Qatar acted to move all of these terrorist groups out of Qatar, out of Doha altogether, where do they go? And to Mr. Goldenberg's point, is there some—is there some benefit to having them there instead of in the arms of ISIS or in Tehran?

Mr. Goldenberg, can you help us sort this out?

Mr. GOLDENBERG. Sure. Thank you, Ranking Member Deutch.

And exactly, I think this is precisely sort of the point. It is com-plicated, but what I would say is—well, maybe I will start with the example of Hamas. And I will actually quote an Israeli former head of research, Josi Kuppelwieser, the former head of research for Israel's military intelligence who has been up here a lot, I believe, also in the past talking about incitements saying, just a year ago publicly, nobody else is ready to help out but Qatar when it comes to Gaza.

So here is a perfect example of the situation we are dealing with. We have had three wars with Israel and Hamas over the few years in Gaza, with large casualties for Palestinians, large casualties for the IDF. And the Israelis have started to realize, well, maybe we should not be—sort of this approach was trying to squeeze Hamas and Gaza doesn't seem to be working. So maybe we need to think about a different approach and trying to at least alleviate the hu-manitarian situation and find ways to quietly establish channels with these guys so as to keep the situation calm and not have an-other conflict.

Who is the only real channel that they have to do that, the Qataris. And so they have been using that channel, and we have been helping in some cases to facilitate that channel. So that is an example.

And so, if Hamas was instead sitting in Tehran, which is a likely outcome of what would happen if they were kicked out of Doha, then I think what you would see is no ability to actually commu-nicate in that way, and probably Hamas taking more aggressive ac-tion and less ability to squeeze them.

So this isn't to justify the Qatari relationship with Hamas. I don't agree with that, necessarily. I think it is a problem. It is not something the U.S. should not have any kind of direct relationship with Hamas. Hamas is a terrorist organization bent on the destruc-tion of Israel. But we sort of found that this approach by the Qataris at least has some benefits, and we should at least recog-nize that as opposed to just vilifying them, because we would like them to behave differently, but at the same time, they end up— when we ask them to do things that sometime are in our interest, they are able to push certain levers we are not able.

Mr. DEUTCH. Dr. Schanzer?

Mr. SCHANZER. Thank you, Congressman Deutch.

I am not even sure where to begin. In terms of the potential ben-efits from Qatar working with Hamas or allowing Hamas to oper-ate out of there, it is sort of a counterfactual. We have yet to actually see what the benefits are, other than the fact that the Israelis have allowed the Qataris to provide assistance to Gaza, not to Hamas, but to the people of Gaza for reconstruction. On that, I think the Israelis would agree that it has been positive. I think we would all agree that it has helped, perhaps, forestall a major humanitarian disaster, and I think for that we should be thankful. But from there, I do have to question.

I mean, it is not like Hamas doesn't have other places where it can operate. It has base in Turkey, for example. It has its home base in the Gaza strip. It operates out of the West Bank. It operates out of Sudan and Lebanon. It has a major presence across the Middle East. Why does it have to operate inside Doha where it gets a certain amount of legitimacy for this?

And then perhaps one other thing to note here is that when people talk about how Qatar may have helped, perhaps, bring the conflict to an end in 2014, if you speak to the other actors in the region, they will tell you, whether it is the Egyptians or the Israelis or even others, they will tell you that is was actually the Qataris and the Turks that forestalled an end to the conflict. That they continued to negotiate on behalf of Hamas, and I think that they probably, in doing so, probably led to the loss of many, many more lives.

Mr. DEUTCH. Unfortunately, I am out of time. Thank you.

I yield back.

Mrs. WAGNER. The gentleman's time has expired.

The Chair now recognizes the gentleman from California, Mr. Cook, for 5 minutes.

Mr. COOK. Thank you, Madam Chair.

In my opening remarks, I talked about this news story about the North Koreans working on a World Cup and figures that I read were about 3,000.

And in the article it talked about the possibility of whether they can be militarized. And this is a scenario that is kind of scary. We talk about the fact that we have our largest military base there, which is, as you said, insane.

Can you just comment on that possibility where this is another dimension, another threat to this? Because every week it seems we have to re-evaluate which is the number one enemy?

Dr. Levitt, could you start?

Mr. LEVITT. So I haven't seen this report, so I don't want to comment on a report I haven't seen, other than to say the North Korea issue is a very important pressing issue. In some ways, it is much more important than this one, to be sure. But in general, I think we need to learn ways to be able to leverage conversation, and if necessary, pressure on Qatar on a wide array of issues that we have with them. And this would be one more. And you have to do that in a way that is flexible, because we have many very positive relationships with Qatar.

I would argue the way to be flexible, though, is not to say it is perfectly okay to have X number of North Koreans in the country working in ways we don't know, or to host anybody you want from Hamas. Certainly, for example, I would make a difference between hosting certain leaders of Hamas who are sitting in a hotel room, as opposed to people like Saad al-Hariri, who is now believed to be in Lebanon but was sitting comfortably in Qatar for quite some time where he was literally plotting attacks against Israelis civilians. That should be completely beyond the pale.

Again, I haven't seen this report, but this would be another thing that we have to figure out how do we have multiple conversations with a country at the same time on some issues you have agreement, on some issues you have great disagreement. I think we have done that very poorly across administrations.

Mr. COOK. Okay. Any others want to comment on this? Doctor?

Mr. SCHANZER. I will comment for a moment, sir. I think it is important to talk about when you talk about foreign workers in Qatar. The 3,000 that you mentioned are actually—it is a very small number, relatively speaking, in relation to this 800,000-plus foreign workers that are active right now in Qatar.

I have seen the reports of the North Korean workers there. The concern actually was not that they would be potentially operational, but rather, that they were effectively slave labor.

Mr. COOK. Yes, exactly.

Mr. SCHANZER. It was given to the Qataris, and that whatever they were being paid was being remitted back to North Korea, and that this was an inadvertent way, or a backdoor way of financing North Korea.

So these are the concerns that we have. I believe that the Qataris have addressed this problem last I heard. I have not seen a lot of updates on this.

Mr. COOK. The reason I ask that question, because we are having the debate and everything else about the sanctions against North Korea, and this might be another variable that would be included in this.

Any comments on what happened last year? I was over in that area, and the State Department was, quite frankly, at that time—this is about a year ago, maybe a year and a half—they were arguing on behalf of Qatar for the upgrade for the F-15s. They thought it would be in the best interest. And I was kind of shocked at that in terms of foreign military sales.

Do you have any comment on that? I almost—when I was there, viewed it as almost Middle East Stockholm syndrome, because they were very, very supportive of Qatar with all its problems, and it kind of shocked me at least from a military standpoint.

Doctor? Either one?

Mr. GOLDENBERG. Sir, I actually had served in the Pentagon for a few years on the Middle East issues, so I can maybe talk a little about this. From my perspective, look, I mean, this is a problem we have with all the Gulf states. On the one hand, I mean, the arm sales are very useful to our industry——

Mr. COOK. Yes. I understand that. But I am talking about the F-15 upgrade. This is a significant—I understand your expertise in the Pentagon. I have spent a few years in the military myself, although I certainly cannot fly an airplane. But in regards to that particular weapon system, which is kind of more sophisticated than some of the others.

Mr. GOLDENBERG. Well, sir, I was just going to say that my issue with—I can't tell you about that specific weapon system, and that specific upgrade. I can tell you that, generally, I think we have an issue where we probably sell these countries too much weaponry because they have the money. And what they really need is, sort of, lower-end technology to deal with counterterrorism problems and things like that, which are much more important, I think, for their interest and ours.

Mr. COOK. Thank you very much. I yield back.

Mrs. WAGNER. The gentleman's time expired.

The Chair now recognizes the gentleman from California, Mr. Lieu, for 5 minutes.

Mr. LIEU. Thank you, Madam Chair.

On June 9, our Secretary of State, Rex Tillerson, stated, "We call on the king of Saudi Arabia, the United Arab Emirates, Bahrain, and Egypt to ease the blockade on Qatar." Later that same exact day, Donald Trump referred to the decision to initiate the blockade as hard but necessary. And then, as you know, a few days later, the United States sells $12 million of fighter jets to Qatar.

So my question is to the panel, what is your understanding of the current U.S. position on this so-called blockade? Do we support it? Do we oppose it? What is the answer to that?

Mr. GOLDENBERG. I will start, I guess. And I think others also have comments.

From my perspective, I think we have a disagreement inside the administration, and for the most part, have seen this disagreement. I am not 100 percent sure. I do think that what it does do, it causes some confusion, because you can't really—Secretary Tillerson is clearly trying to act as a mediator, and he is going out there and trying to do that. He had a trip just last week, or a couple of weeks back to do that. And meanwhile, you have some of these other comments coming from elsewhere, so the Qataris will then go to the Secretary of State, and the Secretary of Defense would seem to have positions more in line with their own, and the Emiratis and the Saudis and others will go the White House, who seems to have positions more in line with their own. And that is really not an effective way to sort of try to conduct and mediate this conflict. I think it is causing some problems.

So I would say it is ambiguous right now what the policy is.

Mr. LIEU. So let me ask you another question. There have been various media reports that the Trump organization has lots of businesses in Saudi Arabia and some of these other countries but not Qatar. Do you think that plays any role, or could it?

Mr. GOLDENBERG. Honestly, Congressman, I don't know. I don't know their motivation, what is behind it.

Mr. LIEU. That is fine. I will ask you another question.

There have been various reports that Jared Kushner basically got stiffed by some folks in Qatar. Do you think this could play any role in that?

Mr. GOLDENBERG. It is certainly a possibility, but it is not something that I, again, have any knowledge of.

Mr. LIEU. Thank you. Let me move on to a question I had mentioned in my opening statement.

Are there families being separated because of this so-called blockade based on their national origin, or any panel member?

Mr. GOLDENBERG. My understanding is at least that, yes, there are issues where the Qataris and the—we have a lot of people who are moving between the Qataris, the Emiratis and the various GCC states, and so you are going to end up in situations where all GC— all, I believe, Qatari nationals had 2 weeks to get out of certain GCC states.

Mr. LIEU. So you would be separating husband and wife from each other if they happen to be a different national origins, correct?

Mr. GOLDENBERG. That is what I have seen in the press. Beyond that, you know—and I have heard concerns about that, but I can't really speak for their policy, obviously.

Mr. LIEU. Okay.

I have met with various representatives from these Gulf state countries, including Saudi Arabia and Qatar. One of the things that the residents from Qatar said is with respect to Taliban, they said it is true there is a Taliban office in Qatar, but that the U.S. asked them to open it. Is that true? Anyone on the panel.

Mr. SCHANZER. I will maybe take a first stab at that one.

As I understand it, there was a Taliban presence that was already there in Doha, that there were representatives of the Taliban who had come there before the opening of this office. Then came the initiative by the Obama administration to negotiate with the Taliban in an attempt to find pragmatic members of the group. And so, they essentially authorized what became the Taliban Embassy.

As I mentioned in my testimony, this was something that was very frustrating to those within the Afghan Government, who were struggling for their own recognition of legitimacy. They felt that this undermined them, and I have heard this from a number of U.S. officials on both sides of the aisle.

What happened after that was the trade for Bowe Bergdahl, the American serviceman who had gone missing in Afghanistan, and he was traded for the Taliban Five. This was facilitated by the Qataris. The Taliban Five are high ranking Taliban officials and operatives, ultimately came to Qatar as well, and so they augmented the presence that had already been there.

And since that time, the concern has been not just that there has been an official presence of the Taliban inside Doha, but rather also Taliban officials, Taliban militants, have come in and they have reconnected with the Taliban Five and some of the others. So there is concern that it is not just that the presence that was first blessed by the Obama administration, but that there have been some operational concerns as well.

Mr. LIEU. Thank you, and I yield back.

Mrs. WAGNER. The gentleman yields back.

The Chair now recognizes the gentleman from New York, Mr. Zeldin, for 5 minutes.

Mr. ZELDIN. Thank you, Madam Chairwoman.

This is a question for anyone who is able to answer. Does Qatar view Hamas as a terrorist organization? Or I can—maybe a multiple choice, or does Qatar view Hamas as a legitimate resistance, or would you give it some other characterization? How does the Government of Qatar view Hamas?

Mr. SCHANZER. Maybe I will start. The Government of Qatar does not see Hamas as a terrorist organization. It sees the violence that Hamas carries out as being legitimate, and it continues to insist that overall, the critique that has been leveled at the Qataris over the last several weeks as this crisis has unfolded, they continue to say that they do not agree with the definition of terrorism that their critics are using.

Again, I see this as a very poor defense. They know exactly how we view the problem, and they are allies of the United States. They are hosting our air base. They know the difference between right and wrong, at least in the way that the West views it, and they refuse to recognize it, and that is one of the problems that we have.

And I think, maybe just a post script, that if this is the case with Hamas, who else might they view differently? How do they view the Taliban? We just talked about the base. How do they view the Nusra front? Do they see them as terrorists? Probably not. And so what we see is a growing list of actors where we would disagree on whether they are legitimate or illegitimate, terrorists or not terrorists.

Mr. ZELDIN. Does anyone disagree with that? What options do we have, if at all, to get Qatar to change their view of Hamas as a legitimate resistance?

Mr. LEVITT. Like in the first instance, there are already reports that Qatar has asked at least six Hamas members to leave the country. That is good. That means some pressure works. So long as there is no consequence, this is a no-brainer for Qatar. Qatar is a small but rich country, and if it wants to box out of its weight class, it can either spend money or do other things that make it more of a player. It has been able to make itself more of a player in part by reaching out to Islamist groups that are beyond the pale for most. And, therefore, being a key intermediary, we collectively, especially coming right after the European Court of Justice's ruling just now upholding the EU's designation of all of Hamas, not some wings and others but all of it, we in the West collectively need to make it clear to Qatar that hosting and providing services to a group that is committed to the destruction of a U.N. member state and to civilians is unacceptable.

And I put that in a different basket from Qatar's support to citizens in Gaza, which the Israelis fully support. In fact, it is done through Israel. That is a different issue. If Qatar wants to be a responsible player in that regard, fine, but hosting and providing safe haven to the leaders of a U.S.- and EU-designated terrorist group is a problem.

Mr. ZELDIN. Has Qatar weighed in, to the best of your knowledge, with regards to the U.S. moving its Embassy from Tel Aviv to Jerusalem? Are you aware of the nature of Qatar helping in the mission to defeat ISIS?

Mr. GOLDENBERG. Well, I think that, yes, in that Qatar hosts, you know, our forces at Al Udeid Air Base, which is where the— you know, we have the CAOC, which is the central coordinating function that then allows—basically is responsible for coordinating all of our operations in Iraq, Afghanistan, and Syria, and especially Iraq and Syria, where ISIS is primarily based, you know as a central element of our strategy, and you know I just would——

Mr. ZELDIN. I really should have clarified. I mean, other than the obvious that, you know, we have a base there, but the nature of these relationships with other terrorist organizations, and they are very welcoming to just about everyone, it seems, in the region.

' So, outside of the obvious, what other—what can we add, what could you add as far as Qatar's other efforts? Not supporting, not allowing us to operate there, but what else are they doing?

Mr. LEVITT. I am not entirely sure I understand the question, but Qatar is a member of the counter-ISIS coalition. Its commitment has been somewhat limited. It has flown some missions, but it has refused to drop bombs, so it has flown behind other airplanes in case something happens to them. That it is not nothing, but it is not as much as others. I think the biggest issue is that now across administrations of different political persuasions we have been more interested in getting another number to add to the number of coalition members adding Qatar without insisting that, to be a part of it, you also have to meet a certain threshold. And it seems crazy to me they should be able to be part of the counter-ISIL coalition while still supporting other equally dangerous radical Islamist groups like al-Qaeda in Syria.

Mr. ZELDIN. I would love to get into that further, but I notice that I am out of time, so I have to yield back.

Mrs. WAGNER. The gentleman yields back.

The Chair now recognizes the gentlelady from Hawaii, Ms. Gabbard, for 5 minutes.

Ms. GABBARD. Thank you.

Thank you, gentlemen.

I am wondering if you can address the double standard that exists and that we are confronted with with all of this attention being focused on Qatar with different members of the administration very strongly calling out Qatar for its support of terrorism, yet on the same—almost in the same breath embracing Saudi Arabia and lauding their counterterrorism efforts, when I think some of you have mentioned in your opening comments Saudi Arabia's long history of supporting terrorism and exporting the Wahhabi Salafist ideology around the world that really creates these fertile recruiting grounds for terrorist groups like al-Qaeda and ISIS—what to speak of Saudi Arabia and Turkey's support of different terrorist groups in places like Syria, Saudi support for al-Qaeda in Yemen and their fight in Yemen. So all of this attention is focused on Qatar with very little if no passing mention of Saudi Arabia's role in all of this.

Mr. SCHANZER. I want to make sure my colleague Matt Levitt gets a moment to speak, but maybe just a couple of quick thoughts. Number one, you mentioned Turkey. I think that probably a whole other hearing should be done on Turkey that the same sorts of behaviors that we are seeing exhibited by the Qataris we have seen with the Turks and we have seen them in very similar ways.

In fact, I think it was just yesterday, I don't know if he is still there, but the President of Turkey, Mr. Erdogan, was in Doha, and they are strategic partners. And I think we need to address this. And I think I mentioned before that the Incirlik Air Base, we have very similar issues with Incirlik that we do with Al Udeid. I see them really as mirror images of one another. The Turks host a Hamas base. They have been known to open up their borders to allow for Nusrah fighters to go back and forth, possibly ISIS fighters, as well, so there is a lot of problems with the Turks that I think probably deserve some attention.

Ms. GABBARD. I agree.

Mr. SCHANZER. Then I think the other thing that both Matt and I mentioned today is the problem of Kuwait. The fact that Kuwait has become a mediator in this is somewhat ridiculous, that the Kuwaitis have been identified time and again by our former and current colleagues at the Treasury Department that Kuwait is a huge problem when it comes to terror finance probably rivaling that of Qatar, and so that should be addressed.

As for Saudi Arabia, I would agree with the assessment that it has turned a corner. It is not out of the woods, but it has gotten a lot better. It is not best in breed. I think that distinction probably goes to the Emirates right now in the Gulf states, but they still have their problems, too.

What I started to say at the beginning of my testimony and prepared remarks is that all of these—the entire Gulf is a problematic region. I think the Saudis were seen as the number one producer of radicalism and radical ideology. I think it has been eclipsed, and as they are trying—it looks as though, right now, they are looking to get better at this. And they still have problems with teaching radicalism and spreading radicalism, but as they improve, we are seeing some of these other countries double down. And Qatar I think has really been the most prominent among them.

Ms. GABBARD. I think—and I have got about a minute and a half if others want to comment—but the issue of Saudi Arabia, we have heard that, yes, they are making progress, and, yes, there is change occurring, but I and others have asked this administration for very specific examples, data, benchmarks, changes, and to date, we have not gotten any kind of specifics, either in writing or in person. And, frankly, what we have gotten is a lot of lip service. So, you know, the question of how long this has been going on with Saudi Arabia casts a huge amount of doubt on saying, yeah, okay, well we think they are improving in this.

Mr. LEVITT. I will just add that Qatar in the here and now, right now, is doing things that have to stop. There is no question——

Ms. GABBARD. I agree.

Mr. LEVITT [continuing]. That the Saudis for a very long time did a whole lot of things that not only caused problems then but are still causing problems now. And I am not going make excuses for them. They have turned corners, and I can't explain why the administration wouldn't provide some information about that, which is not to say that there is not a lot more that they could do.

But as several members of the committee have said, several of you have been approached by different members of GCC states recently, So have those of us in think tanks. And I have mentioned to some of my Saudi and Emirati colleagues in particular: Beware pushing too hard on general ideas of extremism, because it is not like you haven't had problems of your own. Beware of pushing too hard on the issue of the Taliban in Qatar, UAE, because for a period of time, Taliban officials were strolling into Dubai with suitcases of cash, and so long as that was invested in real estate, no one cared.

So the UAE and the Saudis, despite what they have done in the past, have turned corners. We need Qatar to do the same. We shouldn't expect that Qatar will suddenly be perfect in the same way that its neighbors are not yet perfect, but we cannot tolerate some of the most egregious behavior that they have done even, as I said in written and oral testimony, some of the charges that have been arrayed against them are simply untrue, but some of them are very true.

Ms. GABBARD. Thank you.

Mrs. WAGNER. The gentlelady's time has expired.

The Chair now recognizes the gentleman from Florida, Mr. Mast, for, 5 minutes.

Mr. MAST. I want to thank you for taking the time to come here and sit with us today. I want to get to something very quickly. You know, we have been discussing the support of terror from different actors. Terrorism—I have heard it said before, terrorism isn't an enemy. Terrorism is a tactic that is used by an enemy.

So, to that end, I would like to hear from each one of you, what is it that you think is trying to be achieved by the tactic of supporting—by supporting that tactic, by supporting terror? What is the end that each one of you see as being played out?

Mr. LEVITT. So, as answered to another question, I think Qatar is trying to make itself a bigger player in the world stage than it otherwise would be by being a small peninsula, almost an island, of a very small population. A vast majority of people on the island are foreign workers. But it happens to be very, very wealthy, the wealthiest nation on planet earth per capita, and it has also found another way to kind of punch beyond its weight, and that is through making relationships with other Islamist groups that it has been able to use to its own benefit and sometimes being out to reach out to others and say: Hey, I can be a middle man for you too.

That has proved to be very, very dangerous. And so Qatar has never had a situation where there was a cost to having the kind of relationship it wants and needs with us, which we would like to have with them too, at the same time they are having very close relationships with some of the worst of the worst.

Mr. MAST. Mr. Schanzer? Mr. Goldenberg?

Mr. SCHANZER. I agree with Matt. I think that, overall, Qatar realizes that it is extremely vulnerable, that it is tiny, and that it doesn't have the means to push back on some of its very tough neighbors.

It shares natural gas wealth with the Iranians, and they have to figure out how to get along. And so having some of these proxies available to them is a useful thing. By the way, so is having an American air base where they can sort of bare their teeth at the Iranians.

But at the end of the day, what they are trying to do or what has happened over time is they have become very wealthy, and they have tried to use whatever means they have to purchase power. And so you see them buying up large chunks of London, large chunks of Washington. You see them paying for proxies across the Middle East, trying to push the Muslim Brotherhood into positions of power so that they, too, would be able to ride the waves of power. This is a lot of what drives them right now. I think they have taken this way too far.

Mr. GOLDENBERG. And just to add, and I agree a lot of what Jonathan and Matt have said, Qatar is also just traditionally pursued sort of a third way foreign policy in the Gulf. You know, a lot of the smaller Gulf states choose to align themselves with Saudi Arabia. Qatar basically, since 1995, when there was a turnover and a sort of a palace coup and the emir took over, the father of the current emir chose a different approach which involved not just going along with the Saudis. And if you are a very small country with a much bigger one sitting right next to you who sort of is running a lot of the region, if you are going to go with that contrary policy, you try to find every division that you can and every opportunity that you can to influence. And so it builds relationships oftentimes with other actors.

I think this is also is part of the reason they have a slightly different approach to Iran, which is probably a little more accommodationist, although I think that it also has a lot to do with sharing the gas field, as Jonathan said. So I think this is—it is, partially, it is about increasing their influence, but it is also about increasing their influence and being independent of Saudi Arabia within the context of the GCC.

Mr. MAST. Okay. So you have each mentioned what you thought to the end was, and we are talking about terrorism, support of terror. We are talking about a very kinetic action. We are not talking about something cyber. We are not talking about something economic. We are talking about a very kinetic action.

So, in that, being that Qatar has been purchasing foreign military or our military equipment to the tune of $10 billion in 2014, $17 billion in 2015, what is the jump that you make connecting the dots to that end? Do you make a jump there? Do you fear moving from the tactic of terror to a conventional tactic? Is that the assessment that you make?

Mr. LEVITT. No. They are still a small country. They don't want to get into a fight with anybody. I think, in their mind also, this is not a kinetic. They are just supporting groups, and they make a distinction in their own mind this kind of cognitive dissonance between other things they might be doing. They are supporting the political office of Hamas in their mind. They are supporting Islamists who are effective in fighting Assad and nothing else in their mind. It is not quite so simple, but that is what I—I don't think this is at all a threat of regular military-military conflict.

Mr. SCHANZER. I would just add, when you look at Qatar—and we have been having this conversation for the last, you know, hour-plus—I think it is important to note that Qatar is a country of roughly 300,000 people. It is tiny. It has more foreign workers in the country than actual nationals. They are incredibly vulnerable. They are not picking a fight directly with anyone, and this is why they have chosen that soft power approach. They bring the conflict away from them. They cause problems for other people that only they can solve. This is the Qatari way.

Mr. MAST. My time has expired.

Ms. ROS-LEHTINEN [presiding]. Thank you so much, Mr. Mast.

And God has granted me another opportunity to make good on the pronunciation of Mr. Suozzi's name, so I am pleased to yield time to Mr. Suozzi of New York.

Mr. Suozzi. Thank you, Madam Chairwoman.

I am going to pick up on something you just said about 300,000 people that live in Qatar. And I am going to change my line of questioning based on that. There are 1.5 billion Muslims in the world, and the challenge that we face in today's world is—you know, most Muslims don't participate in this awful, horrific activity of terrorism and trying to promote terrorism and extremism and violence, and the challenge is, you know, who is winning in this battle to try and promote extremism and violence? And, you know, there are 750,000 Muslims that live in Indonesia, Pakistan, India, and Bangladesh. The other 750—what did I say 750 million, did I say that? Another 750 million who live outside of those countries.

So the question is: Things are dynamic. Congresswoman Gabbard was talking about, you know, Saudi Arabia's activities over decades and promoting Wahhabism and building madrassas and promoting extremism all over the world, but things are dynamic and things are changing. And some people are moving closer to our way of thinking, not to promote violence and extremism, and some people are moving further away and continuing to promote violence and extremism. So where would you place Qatar on where they are right now?

Mr. Schanzer. It is a great question, and I would say they have got one foot in one camp and one foot in the other. And this is really what is maddening about Qatar. All right. So, on the one hand, they are hosting our forward air base, and they are a vital partner on the war on terrorism, and they are investing through their sovereign wealth. They are investing here in the U.S. and across the West. They are investing in legitimate investments, and they have provided a crucial service in terms of providing hard capital, especially when things got rough about a decade ago; they were there, and they were helping.

The problem is, is that they have used that as leverage. So, when we come to them and we talk to them about their support for the various groups that we have mentioned, the jihadists in Syria, the jihadists in Libya, the Taliban and Hamas, and we go and we talk to them about this, they just don't listen.

Mr. Suozzi. So, if the people from Qatar wanted to clearly demonstrate to us that they are moving away from promoting any kind of extremism and they are moving closer to our way of thinking, the West way of thinking, what would be the two or three things that they would have to do to demonstrate that in a clear way?

Mr. Schanzer. We should be providing Qatar with a list of people that they should expel. It should include people who are part of the Taliban, part of Hamas, part of these various Syrian jihadi groups.

Let me put it this way: I have heard from diplomats in Doha that the Qataris can't do that because it would really upset the Qatari population, that it would really be very unpopular. We are talking about 300,000 people who live in an absolute monarchy. If the emir wants them gone, they will be gone. It is that simple. And we can ask.

Mr. SUOZZI. Okay. I only have 1 minute and 55 seconds left, so Dr. Levitt?

Mr. LEVITT. We are not talking about 300,000 people when we are talking about the problems in Qatar. We are talking about a much, much, much smaller number. In fact, when it comes to the al-Qaeda financiers, we are talking about probably two to three dozen people max that we are truly concerned about. And we are talking about a small number of people in government who need to act.

So this is actually—one of the reasons it is so frustrating is it is so doable. This is an absolute monarchy. They have a respectable security service. They have no tolerance for this type of activity targeting them within the kingdom, but so long as activity that is happening within the kingdom is targeting others, they are okay if it gives them some type of leverage. We need to make clear that there is more leverage to be had in having a wholesome relationship with us, with the Europeans, with the West, and that there are consequences in terms of that relationship if they don't. This is fixable.

Mr. GOLDENBERG. If I can just add one point, Congressman. I think this crisis actually gives us an opportunity to build some leverage and go to all of these countries, to go to the Qataris and say: Okay, here is our list. You really want our support in this crisis? Like we need to see your action on this.

And also to go against the Saudis and the Emirates and—it is the exact same thing.

Mr. SUOZZI. I agree with that.

Mr. GOLDENBERG. And so I think there is this real opportunity now, you know, as sort of the silver lining of this crisis of having our partners all at each other's throats instead of focusing on what we would want to see them focus on because I would rather see them more focused on Iran—I would rather see them focused on the counterISIS fight, not in spending their time in Washington trying to get all of us, you know, on their side—but hereis an opportunity. Let's turn it on them and say: Let's see all of you live up, here is the standard we want to go by, and we want all the countries of the Gulf to go by this standard, and here is what we expect from you.

Ms. ROS-LEHTINEN. Yes, please, go right ahead.

Mr. LEVITT. I realize we are over, but along these lines, there is a mechanism to do that. At the Riyadh summit, we created something called the Terror Finance Tracking Center. There is no meat on those bones yet. No one knows, including the Secretary of the Treasury who just testified about it, no one really knows what that is going to be yet, but it is a potential structure. We could put some meat on those bones. That is a GCC-wide effort, and we should be acting and demanding participation from all the GCC countries because these are problems that are happening within all of them, even if Qatar and Kuwait are the biggest problems right now.

Mr. SUOZZI. So thank you, Madam Chair. You know, there is a real battle in the world going on between stability and instability, and it is not necessarily ideology. It is criminals that are participating in murder and extortion and kidnapping and drug dealing and trying to promote extremism ideology. And it is not a group; it is individuals, as you are pointing out, that we need to target.

Thank you.

Ms. ROS-LEHTINEN. Thank you, sir.

And now we turn to Mr. Issa of California.

Mr. ISSA. Thank you, Madam Chair.

Just for the record briefly, Mr. Schanzer, last time you were in the administration?

Mr. SCHANZER. Ten years ago.

Mr. ISSA. Ten years ago, Bush, right?

So, Levitt, last time?

Mr. LEVITT. Bush.

Mr. ISSA. Mr. Goldenberg, State Department, when?

Mr. GOLDENBERG. 2014.

Mr. ISSA. Okay. So very recently, all facts considered. So all of you have been in a position that this committee oversees. We actually don't oversee Qatar. We don't oversee Kuwait. We oversee the places you were.

So I am going tell you a story. It is a Bush era story. Sixteen years ago there was a hearing in this room, and we were evaluating the incredibly unreasonable activities of Kazakhstan, because they had the audacity to want to sell their MiG-21s to a hostile nation. The other side of the story was they had come to the State Department, they had come to our Government in the Bush administration, and they said: Look, we are a poor country. We are trying to become a rich country. We have got oil. We want to turn—we want to turn these weapons into plowshares. We want to actually sell them off. We are not replacing them. We simply want to raise some cash. And they said: Who can we sell them to?

Mr. Goldenberg, oddly enough, State said: We can't give you a list.

Clearly Lockheed wasn't interested in buying them unless they were trade-ins and neither was Boeing or others.

So my question to you is—each of you—because I have been through these hearings on country after country, and we are going to see whether it is the Palestinian Authority and including Hamas, whether it is Kuwait, Qatar, Saudi Arabia, we are going to keep having these hearings, and we are always going to find one thing. Money is leaking to bad people from within these countries, either by individuals or, in fact, there may be a nexus to the government in some way.

What I want to know is, what are each of you prepared to do and should this administration do under our auspices—and I think, Mr. Schanzer, you alluded to this—to make a list of who you can give to, to make list of who you want out, to make list—in other words, how do we get the administration to set solid, predictable standards, so we know it is not a mixed message, please?

Mr. SCHANZER. Thank you, Congressman. What I would say is, A, I think we can provide lists and say these people shouldn't be here or they should be in jail and that you need to take action. And I think that is a very, you know, straightforward approach. There are other things that I mentioned.

Mr. ISSA. And I will commit that if you provide that list I will forward, and I hope my chairperson will actually do it on my behalf, but I will commit to forward it to the administration asking them, have they and will they make that request?

Mr. SCHANZER. We will take you up on that.

What I would also add, though, is there are other ways of putting pressure on countries like Qatar that don't involve the individuals themselves but that make it more painful. So I mentioned the STORM Act, which was introduced in the Senate.

Mr. ISSA. Right.

Mr. SCHANZER. And is yet to be introduced in the House, but this would potentially label Qatar and/or any other country a jurisdiction of terrorism finance concern, which would then have a chilling effect on those who would be interested in doing commerce.

Mr. ISSA. But my question was more narrow. It is, how do we get, like those lists, specifics to the administration? One of the challenges we have: We pass these various acts, and then there gets to be all kind of debate about it. But what I think I have heard throughout the day, both here and when I was in the back, is that there are specific asks that we should be asking countries to do, including in this case Qatar.

Now there are things that they can't undo. The emir visiting Hamas and giving money for a hospital, we can't unring any of that. We can only feel that it was not helpful, to say the least.

So one of my questions to each of you with the limited time is, can you briefly tell us additional acts, and can you agree to give us lists of things that you believe we should work with the administration to get done? My hope is that it will not be pass a law that ties this and future administration's hands, but, rather, things you know should be done that we need to ask them, why aren't they doing it?

Mr. LEVITT. So to be perfectly blunt, sir——

Mr. ISSA. I love blunt.

Mr. LEVITT. I know you do. They know, because we have told them. I am happy—I will speak for all three of us. We are happy to provide you information. We have a Treasury attache in Doha. He works real hard all the time. This new MOU is going to send a Department of Justice OPDAT official, a prosecutor, to help them with the prosecutions. There is no question about the names, not only because we have designated many, because we have this very open conversation with them many times. In one of my recent conversations with the senior Qatari official, the official said to me: Look, Matt, you are former FBI. We need the FBI to tell us.

I said: No, sir. You have a really good security service. I know because I have worked with you in the past. I know that our people are working with you on a regular basis. You know that I know that you know exactly who we are talking about.

And, therefore, it is frustrating, as I mentioned earlier, when a senior Qatari official says just yesterday: All of the terror financier subjects in our country have been subject to prosecution.

That is not true, nor is prosecution the only tool in the tool chest.

So I would argue that the problem here is not the lists. The problem here is that they refuse to do it, and we haven't had any type of consequence for that because we need them for other things. We want them for other things, but we have to be able to balance that.

Mr. Issa. Well, that is why I believe our list forwarded will have more of a, why not?

And I want you to answer, but my question was broader. It wasn't just Qatar. It is very clear that we have similar requests from other allies or semi-allies throughout the Gulf, yes.

Mr. Goldenberg. Thank you, Congressman. Just one quick point. I know we are over time, but I think one thing the committee could do is, for example, ask for a report on what it would mean to actually diversify away from the Qatari air base, not because I necessarily recommend doing that. I actually think it would end up being very expensive and difficult, and if we can, we should could keep that base. It is a valuable asset. But I also don't think it is a point of leverage to the point that we just mindlessly say, "Well, we are just going to keep doing this because we are doing it right now," and it keeps a gun to our head. And I think, unless you sort of push the Pentagon or the State Department to at least start creatively thinking about alternatives, the answer you will always get from any administration is, "We have zero leverage here, we need this space," which is isn't actually the case. So that would be another area which would also I think send an interesting——

Mr. Issa. Thank you, Madam Chair.

Ms. Ros-Lehtinen. Thank you, Mr. Issa.

And now we turn to Mr. Cicilline of Rhode Island.

Mr. Cicilline. Thank you, Madam Chairman.

Thank you to our witnesses for your testimony.

Dr. Levitt, I just want to just start with you. You served as Deputy Assistant Secretary of the Treasury and so you understand the critical role that our agencies play in advancing and implementing U.S. foreign policy, and as I am hearing your testimony, it just reminds me how disturbing it is and how much more complicated it is that this administration has not only called for a 30-percent cut in funding to the State Department but has left really important positions vacant and without nominees. At a moment that we are trying to manage this crisis and this very serious conflict in the Middle East, we are still waiting on nominees for the Assistant Secretary for Near Eastern Affairs and USAID Assistant Administrator for the Middle East, and at a time when terror groups continue to talk about efforts to pursue weapons of mass destruction, it is really baffling to me that we would leave vacant the position of Under Secretary for Arms Control and International Security. I take it you all are equally mystified by that?

Mr. Levitt. It would be much better if we had these positions filled.

Mr. Cicilline. Great. Thank you.

I want to first talk about Turkey. One of the demands on Qatar has been to close the Turkish military base located in Qatar, and Turkey has responded, of course, by bolstering its military presence as a strong show of support. And my question really is, is this a real demand? What is the purpose of it? And what would be the implications if this base closed?

Mr. Schanzer. I will let Ilan speak in a sec, but what I would just say is you have to understand: We talk about the politics of this region, and overall, these countries are upset with Qatar for its financing of Muslim Brotherhood groups across the Arab world.

And they see it as a challenge to their view of the region, in which they would like to maintain something of the status quo. The Turks have been strategic partners with the Qataris. There is no question about it. And so they see this as doubling down on that sort of Muslim Brotherhood Axis, if you will, and so they see it as a threat. I don't think they want to open up another front on this. I think they are focusing on Qatar for a reason, but when you speak to representatives of these countries, they will tell you that they see the Turks as perhaps second in line in terms of a challenge to the regional order that they seek.

Mr. CICILLINE. And is your assessment that this has pushed Qatar closer to Turkey, this blockade?

Mr. SCHANZER. Oh, they didn't need to be any closer. They were already strategic partners, but now I think—I mean, as I see it right now, Qatar has very few friends, so they have reached out to the Turks, and they have drawn closer to the Turks. And alarmingly, they also appear to have drawn closer to the Iranians, which is one of the things that Qatar's adversaries were warning about in the first place.

Mr. GOLDENBERG. Congressman, if I can add one point on Turkey, there was this initial list of 13 demands by the countries that implemented the blockade. That list has since been narrowed down to six and was last week in a statement that they put out, and the Turkish base is no longer on that list of demands. And so I think that the Turkey issue is an issue for them precisely for the reasons that Jonathan talked about, but it is, I think, a lesser priority for them than some of the issues on counterterror financing, their concerns about whether Qatar's meddling in their own internal affairs, which they consistently talk about Al Jazeera, things like that I think really what they care alot more about than the Turkey issue.

And on Iran, I would only add I think it is true that, yeah, Qatar has a more accommodationist approach than some of the other Gulf states, but I think there is a real mix across the Gulf on Iran that is important to recognize. The GCC—if anything, we have learned from this crisis, the GCC is not homogeneous. The Saudis take the hardest line on Iran. Even within the UAE, Abu Dhabi takes a hard line; Dubai much less so in terms of trade. So, you know, I do think there is this diversity of views. Oman obviously played a very different role on Iran, more as a mediator, particularly during the nuclear talks.

Mr. CICILLINE. I would like to follow up on Iran. The Qataris have obviously been trying to counter Iran's strategically while at the same time trying to kind of continue to maintain a dialogue with their Iranian counterparts. What do you think is the rationale for that decision and the kind of long-term implications?

Mr. GOLDENBERG. So I think they are a country of 300,000 people, as we have talked about, and all of their wealth—the majority of their wealth comes from this huge gas field that they share with the Iranians. You know, they own half of it; the Iranians have the other half. So this is a reality of geopolitics that they are living with, and you are never going to get them to, I think, pull away completely.

At the same time, at least my engagement with Qatari Government officials, you don't hear a lot of love for the Iranians necessarily. You do hear some angst, but they are not going to take a hard-line approach like the Saudis. I just don't think they can afford to, given like the position that they are in.

Mr. SCHANZER. I would agree with that. I think a lot of this is driven by the Qatari need for survival. But I have heard from some of our friends in the region in recent months a concern that the Muslim Brotherhood and Iran are not exactly at odds with one another. I think we have this sort of preconceived notion that, because the Muslim Brotherhood is a Sunni organization, a Sunni network, it is fundamentally at odds with Iran. That has not been the case historically. Looking just at Hamas, for example, you have this confluence of both Qatari support and Iranian support there, so there may be more than meets the eye, and this is, I think, something that is worthy of perhaps additional research.

Mr. CICILLINE. Thank you so much.

I yield back.

Ms. ROS-LEHTINEN. Thank you so much, Mr. Cicilline.

Mr. Rohrabacher of California.

Mr. ROHRABACHER. Thank you very much, and I appreciated your insights that you have provided us today. I have got a long history in dealing with Qatar and with those other countries. I have been here 30 years now, and I worked with the White House before I got here.

And what I—I can't help but lament that things seem to be going in the opposite direction than what we had as a positive potential 20 and 30 years ago. It really did look like Qatar and some other countries in that region were going to go in a more positive direction, and now what we see is basically they are—schizophrenia on their part trying to play both sides against all sides, or these people think that they can just juggle. They think they are the world's greatest jugglers in that they can handle both groups of enemies and friends.

So let me ask this: When you talk to the people from Qatar, and I have, and they will tell you every time that they—and, again, one other—there was one question earlier on this—that they were asked to bring in the Taliban, that they were asked to bring in al-Qaeda and Hezbollah and these various groups, by the United States Government. Did—even during the last administration, did we indeed ask them to bring in the Taliban and have a greater opportunity for the Taliban to use their area there in Qatar as a base of dealing with the world?

Mr. GOLDENBERG. So I didn't work—I was in the last administration, but I did not work on issues having to do with the Taliban.

Mr. ROHRABACHER. Can anyone answer that question? They are telling us we asked them to do it. Did we ask them to do it?

Mr. GOLDENBERG. But I do think—I can answer, from my understanding, which is I do think we asked them to do it, but I do think it also goes back to this point that part of the reason we asked them to do it is because the Taliban were already operating there in some form or capacity already.

Mr. ROHRABACHER. So there is some verification that perhaps the United States Government did ask them to get involved with some of these what we consider to be terrorist elements. We know that the deal for the Taliban Five leaders, terrorist leaders, were traded for one traitor to our Government, and which I thought was the worst raw deal that we could have ever possibly have gotten, that was something our administration did, and it would happen via Qatar.

Now, let me just ask this, and I am going to be very pointed here, and, look, the Clinton Foundation has received millions of dollars of contributions, we know, from Russian oligarchs. Is there any—how much has the Clinton Foundation received from Qatar? Do we know of any—or maybe Qatar has not given any money to the foundation. Is that right?

Mr. LEVITT. None of us have those figures, but I just want to correct one thing. There is some debate as to what the United States might have asked Qatar to do or not regarding the Taliban, and I think it is now clear. They asked Qatar to allow this office to be open since the Taliban was already there, but this was not Hamas. You had mentioned Hamas. This was not Hezbollah. This was not al-Qaeda.

Mr. ROHRABACHER. I am sorry. I have 1 minute left, and let me just note, Madam Chairman——

Ms. ROS-LEHTINEN. You have more time. Don't worry about it.

Mr. ROHRABACHER. Okay. Well, I think it would be fitting, Madam Chairman, that we make a request to find out if Qatar has been the source of major donations to the Clinton Foundation, and if, indeed, our Government, during the time when Hillary Clinton was our Secretary of State, did indeed ask Qatar to permit some of these what we consider terrorist organizations into their country. This needs to be looked at very closely because we know that the Clinton Foundation was certainly in Russia receiving tens of millions of dollars from Russian oligarchs.

Let's just note that whether it is al-Qaeda or the Muslim Brotherhood, the jihadists and Hezbollah, Qatar has to make its choice. And by the way, just one point that was made here earlier: I do not consider the rebuilding of Gaza to be a positive act. If, indeed, the Palestinians are shooting rockets into Israel and Israel retaliates, for Qatar just to step forward and to rebuild everything that has been destroyed by Israeli retaliation, what we are really doing is encouraging the people in Gaza to permit the shooting of rockets from their territory into Israel.

No, the fact is that, if, indeed, Israel is retaliating against an attack, we should not be cleaning up the mess. Those people who actually permitted the attacks in the first place should be paying a price for it. Because we don't want attacks. We want there to be peace. This is the two-state solution was supposed to come out of this, and instead, the Palestinians ever since then have just been shooting rockets and creating terrorist attacks against Israel. Now let's discourage that by not rebuilding their buildings if they have been destroyed as a retaliation against this type of terrorist attack on Israel.

Let me just say again, and I agree with this, that this has not been a hearing about all the rest of these states. Frankly, I don't find Qatar any worse than our Saudi friends, and there is, again, schizophrenia going on there. But we look at the Muslim Brotherhood and the impact that it is having throughout that region, and we realize that, both in Qatar and in Saudi Arabia, they embrace the Muslim Brotherhood philosophy, which has served as basically the intellectual foundation for these terrorists, wherever they are, whatever you want to call them, al-Qaeda or Hezbollah or jihadists or Taliban or whatever we want to call them, ISIL. We need to make sure—it is a time of choosing right now that the juggling has got to stop, and I would hope that the royal family in Qatar and the people of Qatar decide to be our friends because they have that choice, but if they continue down this path, they will be deciding not to be our friends and decide instead with the Muslim Brotherhood and the terrorists. So I hope that this hearing today sends that message.

Ms. Ros-Lehtinen. Thank you.

Thank you, Mr. Rohrabacher.

And Mr. Schneider is recognized for the same amount of time.

Mr. Schneider. Thank you, Madam Chairwoman. I will apologize in advance, I have a concurrent markup in judiciary. If I jump up and leave, it is because I have to go vote. Please don't take it personally. But thank you for your time here for sharing your perspectives, but also for the work you do on this and other important issues.

There is so much here and so much to understand. I think my colleagues have touched on some of the intuitive and counterintuitive aspects of our relationship with Qatar and the difficulties in fully defining the parameters. I will ask a leading question. Would it be better for us and the region if Hamas, the Taliban, al-Qaeda weren't raising finances in Doha?

Mr. Levitt. Yes, it would be better.

Mr. Schneider. Dr. Schanzer?

Mr. Schanzer. Yes, it would, and it would also be better if they didn't have a presence there that was legitimized.

Mr. Schneider. Mr. Goldenberg?

Mr. Goldenberg. Yes.

Mr. Schneider. And the reason I ask the question is you can make lemonade out of lemons. You can find, in a difficult or a bad situation, something to pull out of it, but I think what I am hearing is a broad consensus that we are looking to the Qataris to end the financing of terror in their country and to be a full partner in fighting terrorism in the region. Is that a fair summary?

Mr. Levitt. It is, but I think it is just as important to that we finish off today by noting that we need the other GCC countries, this kind of coalition of four in particular to be flexible and allow Qatar some face-saving ways to do this. And so far, they seem to be pretty kind of hardline that nothing is good enough. And so we absolutely must demand that Qatar make real substantive and verifiable change, but in order for that to happen, we are going to have to have, you know, honest conversations with our other allies in the region and kind of insist that they be flexible enough to find a way that Doha can do this, and that is going to have to involve some face-saving gestures, and that is okay so long as the changes are substantive and verifiable.

Mr. Schneider. Thank you.

And that is where I was trying to get to. So I appreciate that sentiment because it is a matter of we have a base in Qatar. It is an important base to the work we are trying to do in the region.

The work we are doing is longitudinal. It is not going to be solved overnight, and we need to have a long-term strategy.

Mr. Goldenberg, you referenced and others did, as well, the issue that we have options to look at other places besides Qatar to place our assets, and to the whole panel, as you look at the region, what would be the benefits to us to having a more diverse platform, diversified platform, than just the base in Qatar?

Mr. GOLDENBERG. I think there is definitely, Congressman, a benefit—there is always a benefit to having more diverse options. We have other options in the region. We have options in Central Asia. We have a base in the UAE. We have a base in Bahrain. So the more options you have, the less leverage any one of these actors has over us. At the same time, I think we would have to do a real evaluation because if we lost the base in Qatar, I mean, they even invested $1 billion in that base during the nineties. That is a ton of money. They do have technology there and sort of runways and space and things we don't necessarily have elsewhere.

And so I think it would be—and on top of that, if you end up in a situation where we lose access to the base, then you also start running into questions of not being able to conduct as many operations in Iraq, in Syria, and Afghanistan and elsewhere and also a problem where we could bring in a carrier or something like that to offset some of those problems, but then you lose the ability to do things in the Asia Pacific or in Europe. So it is a very complicated question, but it is worth—it is certainly worth exploring, instead of making it just a sacred cow, because whenever you make something a sacred cow and it becomes invaluable to you, then you have a lot less leverage over everything else.

One other point, if I can just add on to what Matt was saying, which I think is just important to also weigh, I really do think we need to focus on getting all of our friends in the region to deescalate this crisis, because you just go back and look at it: You know, the President went in May, and the whole conference in Riyadh was about ISIS, Islamic extremism, and Iran. And what have we been doing for 2 months now with these guys? What is Secretary Tillerson doing when he goes out for a week to the GCC? What are we talking about here today? We are talking about the fight they are having amongst each other.

You know, if they are spending 90 percent of their time, which I have had diplomats telling me, "I am spending 90 percent of my time on this issue," you know, they are not spending time thinking about all of the other things we want them to think about and what we want to think about. So I think that is a really important piece of trying to deescalate this and trying to find a solution, even as we push them on the terrorism.

Mr. SCHNEIDER. Thank you. I think that is an important point.

My last line is, as we are doing that, as we are balancing all these different issues, consistency of message on our part, transparency on the part of the Qataris, what is the impact of the divergent message or inconsistent messages coming out of the administration having on our ability to move forward in this region?

Dr. Schanzer.

Mr. SCHANZER. I think it is clear that we have a couple of different messages that are coming out. We are hearing, on the one hand, that this crisis is not an urgent issue for the administration and, at the same time, that it is something that we do want to have handled.

I think perhaps some of the actors in the region believe they have a free hand to act when they hear parts of the administration speak and then perhaps feel more constrained. I think consistency is going to be important here. I personally believe that we should be sending a message to the Qataris that we demand change. And that ought to be the first thing that we say and then to follow up with that by saying: And as we demand this change of you, the other four actors involved in this crisis can stand down while we take over.

And that I think would be the way to get this to a soft landing and perhaps would be one of the face-saving sort of mechanisms that Matt discussed here today. But I would like to see more American leadership on this, if possible.

Mr. SCHNEIDER. To use your analogy, though, as well, the Ferrari and the other car is also speeding. Is it fair to say that we need to have expectations of all of our allies in the region that they are addressing the terror issue?

Mr. SCHANZER. 100 percent.

Mr. SCHNEIDER. Okay. Dr. Levitt, to you.

Mr. LEVITT. I just say, in my conversations with officials of the past few weeks, it is very clear that the conflicting messages coming out of the administration are affecting them. I have spoken to people on both sides of this intra GCC conflict, and each clearly feel that they can listen to the part that is saying what they want to hear. I have also been in Europe recently and in conversations with counterterrorism officials there, they have been asking me—and I am no longer a government official—what does Washington really think? And so our allies are confused as to what our position is.

I think there are other ways that we can do face-saving gestures. I think Jonathan is absolutely right. If we play more of a role, there is more likelihood that things will move forward. We just agreed on a memorandum of understanding with Qatar. Again, there is not a lot of meat on the bones of that. That is fine. Let this be a mechanism to which we say, through guarantees to us—and let's bring others in, the EU others—Qatar is going to make the following changes. Qatar has to be willing to agree to make those changes and to do it in verifiable ways, and then we can go to the Emiratis and the Saudis in particular and say: Hey, this is how it is going to be done, and this is what the verification is going to look like.

But the Qataris have to be willing to make those changes and to do it in such a way that will be verifiable.

Mr. SCHNEIDER. Great. I see that I am out of time. I appreciate the extended time. I do agree we do have to be clear in our expectations, clear in our strategy in working with all our allies in the region.

Thank you very much. I yield back.

Ms. ROS-LEHTINEN. Thank you, Mr. Schneider. Mr. DeSantis of Florida.

Mr. DESANTIS. I thank the chairman.

Dr. Schanzer, how would you describe Qatar's relationship with Iran?

Mr. SCHANZER. Uneasy. Although also a bit more ambiguous than perhaps what has been previously described. Uneasy in the sense that they are a small country, they are a weak country, and they are looking across the Persian Gulf at a powerful country that is on the precipice of a nuclear weapon, and they need to figure out a way to get along with this neighbor, especially one where they share this natural gas field.

So that I think explains in general the dynamic, but we have been hearing that there could be more cooperation than was previously seen. I mean, this is essentially what the Gulf quartet has been alleging against Qatar, that it has been working with the Iranians or perhaps with its proxies. I have heard allegations, not just of Hamas, where we know there has been sort of, you know, a cooperation on all fronts, but also potentially Hezbollah, potentially the Houthis in Yemen. We have heard these things. There is not a lot of evidence yet to prove these things, but it is certainly something worth watching.

Mr. DESANTIS. There are also reports I think that Qatari money has ended up in Iraq with some of the Iranian-backed militia groups there?

Mr. SCHANZER. Correct.

Mr. DESANTIS. What about the Muslim Brotherhood and the relationship that Qatar has with the Brotherhood? I read your testimony, and you had wrote about some of the people that they were—Qatar was really supportive of the Morsi government in Egypt after Mubarak was pushed out, but then when General el-Sisi took over, that Qatar was kind of a haven for some of these people, and I have heard reports that some of these really radical clerics like Sheikh Qaradawi, who is one of the biggest Muslim Brotherhood clerics, is in Qatar. So is that true, a lot of those folks who were involved with the Brotherhood government now have refuge in Qatar?

Mr. SCHANZER. A hundred percent, and in the previous Gulf crisis, there was one 3 years ago, one of the demands of Qatar was that they exile some of these Muslim Brotherhood figures, that they expel them from the country. But when you look at what the Qataris invested in Egypt during that 1 year plus of Morsi rule, it was reportedly $18 billion. It was a real significant investment. You look their support for various actors in Syria; they were definitely throwing their weight behind the Brotherhood there. In the early years of the uprising, the Ennahda Party in Tunisia. Qataris are big supporters there. The Muslim Brotherhood in Libya. It is I think at this point undeniable that the Qataris are the number one supporter financially and politically of the Muslim Brotherhood in the Muslim world. I think Turkey is probably number two, not as much financially but more politically, although perhaps a bit of both. But this is really the cornerstone of the debate as I see it between Qatar and its neighbors, that the neighbors are furious because they do not want to see the Muslim Brotherhood come to power, and they believe that the Qataris have continued to finance and support the Brotherhood in many theaters.

Mr. DeSANTIS. So what is their reason for doing that? I mean, there it is a very wealthy country, the—I mean, just the royal family, huge wealth. Is it just idealogically that is what they want to do because it seems like it has caused them a lot of problems in the region.

Mr. SCHANZER. I agree it has caused them problems, and I would say that, at this point, when you look at what has happened throughout this crisis, it looks like a gamble that has not paid off, and I think many of the other gambles throughout the Arab Spring, it looks like a lot of money has effectively gone to waste, but they see this as their leverage, a counterleverage to their Gulf neighbors with whom they have a pretty significant rivalry, and it is their way of I think punching above their weight, as Matt had mentioned, and so they continue to pursue this.

I think there is certainly an ideological approach here, though, as well.

Mr. DeSANTIS. I am sorry. I actually have run out of time, but do you guys have any insights into the Brotherhood relationship, or did he cover everything?

Mr. GOLDENBERG. I mean, I think, as Jonathan described, there is this relationship. It is a long historical relationship. I think—you know, I am more skeptical about how much of it is ideological and how much of it is more just geopolitical playing, you know, the Qatari overall third way. You know, if it was really deeply ideological, why would they also build a strong relationship with us at the same time? To me, it is more of like they don't want to play the same role, they don't want to just follow the Saudis, they want to be an independent actor in the Gulf. So they are going to just pursue an open-door policy that welcomes all kinds of different players, some of which we can work with, including ourselves, some of which are a huge problem. And so that is the motivation. It doesn't necessarily explain the behavior which—or excuse the behavior, which I think, again, sometimes they can be useful to us on some of these things, but a lot of times, we need to press them harder to stop.

Mr. DeSANTIS. I am out of time, and I will yield back.

Ms. ROS-LEHTINEN. Thank you so much, Mr. DeSantis.

Sheila? And now we are so pleased that two members who are not on our subcommittee, but I know that they are very interested in this issue, and I am very pleased to yield to them, and we will start with Ms. Jackson Lee of Texas.

Ms. JACKSON LEE. Let me thank the chairwoman for her leadership and the ranking member for their leadership of this committee and the important testimony that has been given by the witnesses. I am in the same predicament. Though I have been able to listen to the testimony for a while, I am in the markup and may be called to a vote as I speak. But I will rush very quickly to thank the witnesses.

But I really want to speak to Mr. Goldenberg, if I might. I notice that the title of the hearing is "Assessing the U.S.-Qatar Relationship," which I think is extremely important. So, if you might bear with me, I am going to ask questions more or less in a lawyerly factor.

Would you indicate or confirm that—and I am just going to go back as far as the Clinton administration, the Bush administration and Obama—in those administrations, would you venture to say that Qatar engaged positively with the United States in Bill Clinton? I am just going to get you, yes or no.

Mr. GOLDENBERG. Yes.

Ms. JACKSON LEE. Mr. George W. Bush?

Mr. GOLDENBERG. Yes.

Ms. JACKSON LEE. And President Obama?

Mr. GOLDENBERG. Yes.

Ms. JACKSON LEE. So, if you just wanted a blanket assessment, that was a positive relationship between the United States and Qatar on some of the issues they were discussing?

Mr. GOLDENBERG. I would say yes. I would say that they are—you know, look I think, Congresswoman, I think that we have a good relationship with them on a number of issues, the most important I think being the air base, but beyond that, you know, when we ask them to do things, they often do them.

Ms. JACKSON LEE. And let me—forgive me, I am called to a vote. During the Bush administration, do you have a recollection or by news or your research that then Secretary of State asked them to engage with Hamas?

Mr. GOLDENBERG. I don't know, but one of my colleagues might know better than me.

Ms. JACKSON LEE. Okay. So you mentioned or in the discussion, we have mentioned that the region is an important region. I, from the lawyer's perspective, say that none of them in the court of equity are there with totally clean hands, and I would offer to say that stability is important. Security is important. And in your testimony, I would like you to repeat what you said about engaging so that we can encourage the stability—I understand the list has now been in essence pared down to about six of the demands, but how would it be best for us to effectuate that engagement where all of the parties recognize that there are elements of their policy dealing with terrorists that should be eliminated?

Mr. GOLDENBERG. Sure. I mean, I think that the most important thing—and Matt's brought this up a couple times during the hearing, this question of the MOU being a good starting point. Setting one bar for everyone to meet on the question of terror financing would be, I think, very valuable because there is—the Kuwaitis are a problem. The Qataris are a problem. Maybe the Saudis are getting better, but there is a long history there and a long way to go. The UAE has also had its issues. And so holding them all and saying the United States will hold them all to one standard and applying that standard across all of them I think becomes beneficiary to us in terms of dealing with the overall challenge and also helps to alleviate this crisis amongst them. And then I think also just in terms of dealing with stability and dealing with the region, it is really hammering home the point that we are not going to want to like want to spend all of our time dealing with this internecine conflict that they have amongst themselves. It is time to get back to the bigger issues that threaten their stability and threaten our stability, you know, the things that really draw us into the region, and whether that is ISIS, you know, extremism, you know, some of the things that Iran does in the region that are problematic, but that is where I would really like to see the relationship——

Ms. JACKSON LEE. So any interjection by Congress for placing punitive measures on one of the other, in this instance, maybe Qatar, would you view that as a positive act?

Mr. GOLDENBERG. I wouldn't recommend doing that. I would recommend having a standard that Congress applies to everyone across the board. And Qatar might—you know, as Jonathan said, you know, that analogy, Qatar might have the fastest—you know, might be the 90 miles per hour Ferrari, and so they are going to have longer to go.

Ms. JACKSON LEE. And let me follow-up with, I think, almost concluding question. Emboldening one over the other, I happened to have been in the region during the visit of the administration, and meeting with, at that time, the President of Egypt and discussing these issues. I have a very strong commitment to the region for its security relationship to Israel, which we want to ensure their safety. And would you make the argument that, as you just said, focusing our attention on the larger picture, and trying to ensure the stability of the region by way of setting a certain standard, would that be helpful in terms of making sure the region remains stable for other big fights, and, also, the security of Israel?

Mr. GOLDENBERG. Yeah, I think it would, and I think also, Congresswoman, you mention the issue of emboldening. I do think that—you know, we made a mistake by essentially signaling a green light and a blank check to the Saudis with the President's visit to the region, and basically led them to believe that there was nothing they could do wrong, so they did this. Where the stronger message I think would have been, you know, we will take a tougher stance on the issues you care about, whether it is Iran—or I would not advocate for walking away from the nuclear deal. I think we should stick to the nuclear deal. But, you know, you want to take a harder stance toward Iran's behavior in the region, you want us to do more on counterterrorism, we will do that, but we also expect you to clean up some of your act. And we have expectations of you. This isn't a blank check. This is a quid pro quo or an agreement between a relationship between two partners. And so I think that was part of the problem out of that trip.

Ms. JACKSON LEE. Let me thank the chairlady——

Thank you all for your testimony. Forgive me for my focused questioning. But let me thank of the chairlady for her kindness. And I like the blank-check analysis that we should not give, and that we should work together for harmony—I like that word as well—in the region. I thank you so very much, and I yield back to the gentlelady.

Ms. ROS-LEHTINEN. Thank you. We are thrilled that you were able to join us.

And Mrs. Maloney, if you could hold your fire for a just few minutes, because Mr. Connolly, who is on our subcommittee, is back with us, so we are going to yield time to him right now.

Mr. Connolly of Virginia.

Mr. CONNOLLY. I thank the chair.

Mr.—Dr. Schanzer, when you were—in your opening statement, you made some allusion to—a reference to maybe paid lobbyists for governments in the region had descended on our offices or paid a visit. I am not sure I understood the point of that, or what you were getting at, but I wanted to give you an opportunity to explain. Because, I mean, there are a lots of lobbyists, for lots of countries, including Israel, that descend on our offices, and we don't necessarily import to that anything negative by way of inference. Were you suggesting——

Mr. SCHANZER. No, Congressman Connolly. There is nothing illegal or unseemly about it. I think the point that I am trying to make is that there is a lot of it right now.

Mr. CONNOLLY. That what?

Mr. SCHANZER. There is a lot of it right now. There is a lot of noise. We are seeing a lot of different actors.

Mr. CONNOLLY. I am sorry, because I only have—do you mean about Oman—excuse me, Qatar?

Mr. SCHANZER. About this Qatar conflict. But I think in general, when we look at the permissive nature of what we have allowed to take place across this region, in my view, it has been the direct result of yielding to these actors. In other words, over time, this has become sort of the boiling frog, although I heard the other say that actually is not scientific, that frogs actually can be boiled. They won't jump out.

But regardless, what I would say is that over time, we have come to just accept the fact that there are terror financiers running around in Qatar, that there are terror financiers running around in Kuwait, and we are being asked to look the other way. And over time, we have grown used to this because they have engaged with us on deals to buy weapons, on investments here in the United States, and because they have a face here in Washington. And what I would like to do is to try to look beyond the messaging and get back to the facts here, which is that we have problematic relations.

Mr. CONNOLLY. Right. But could it not also be because we also have bases? Could we have troops stationed there? And we have the largest base in the region in Qatar?

Mr. SCHANZER. We do. And the question——

Mr. CONNOLLY. I mean, maybe we have conflicting interests here. I am not testifying to that behavior, but it is not a simple matter of paid lobbyists who are influencing us here, there is a lot of money flowing around. It is because, actually, we are looking at U.S. interest in the region, and we see a conflict.

Mr. SCHANZER. But I would actually argue in response to that that one of the reasons why we have been able to keep the base, or how the Qataris have been able to keep that base, is that we continue to hear, Well, gosh, they are doing all these wonderful things, and they are helping us out. So, you know, we will deal with this terror finance problem quietly over here. Let's not deal with it. Now, look 10 years later, and we still have this problem. We now have a full-blown crisis.

My argument is, is that we have not dealt honestly with the problem of terrorism finance in Qatar for a long time, and I would argue that we probably haven't dealt honestly with the terror finance problems of some of those other countries as well.

Mr. CONNOLLY. Yeah, I—I mean, if we are going to go that route, I would add to your list. I mean, I would add the Saudis, financing Wahhabism and madrassahs all over the world that have fomented enormous amounts of terrorism and extremism, one can argue.

Okay.

Mr. Goldenberg, you talked about the conflicting messages from the President and Secretary of State with respect to this conflict. And I have to agree with you. I am just wondering, adding to that, like, what is the policy? And should we be doing it by tweet? Different. But how about the State Department, only two of 22 Assistant Secretaries even nominated, the Ambassador in Doha resigning and arguing because increasingly, it is difficult to wake up overseas and try to explain what the hell is going on in Washington, DC, and what it means as the Ambassador. And of course, a proposed 32 percent cut to State and aid, just spitballing here, could that have something to do with our inability to effect some kind of understanding and agreement and reconciliation among the GCC?

Mr. GOLDENBERG. Well, I will say this: Yes, I think it is a huge problem that you have all these vacancies. And it is a good example of the fact that Secretary Tillerson had to go over there on his own for 4 days.

I am not sure I would have recommended that. I don't think this issue necessarily merits that, unless you actually think you are going to have some agreement, or unless you are going to have some kind of a breakthrough. And it is very obvious to those of us watching it, that you weren't going to have an agreement.

So I do think that in a situation like that, who else do you send, though? You pretty much have nobody, especially the Assistant Secretary. As you know, somebody who worked for the State Department for a number of years.

You know, in every department and in every agency, and I have worked in a couple, there is that key level in the middle, that the individual who is senior enough to be able to reach up to the Secretary of State and, like, get in front of them immediately and inform them, and still close enough for the worker bees and the people working, and the experts in the agency who can reach down and pull in.

At the State Department, those are the Assistant Secretaries. They are the key, in my view, node. And the fact that they don't exist means there is no connectivity between the entire Department and the expertise and the Secretary.

So, yes, I think it harms us on this issue, and pretty much all issues.

Mr. CONNOLLY. And, Madam Chairman, Lois Frankel had a question. If I could ask it on her behalf and that way——

Ms. ROS-LEHTINEN. Yes, we would be honored to have you ask it on her behalf.

Mr. CONNOLLY [continuing]. We shave 5 minutes, you know?

Ms. ROS-LEHTINEN. Please go ahead.

Mr. CONNOLLY. All right.

So Lois' question, Ms. Frankel's question, and I will put it to you first, Mr. Goldenberg: Would the removal of our military base give license to or make worse the behavior in question?

Mr. GOLDENBERG. It is an interesting question. I hadn't thought about it precisely that way.

It may. I think the—I think the bigger challenge logistically would be that if we were to remove the military base, we—it would, first of all, be incredibly costly. The Qataris spent $1 million on that base. Yet, look at what the alternatives are. It would then strain our ability to conduct operations, the same tempo in Iraq, Afghanistan——

Mr. CONNOLLY. I don't think that is the question. I think the question is——

Mr. GOLDENBERG. By leverage.

Mr. CONNOLLY [continuing]. Implied here, by having the military base in Qatar, does it moderate behavior? Would it be worse without it, assuming there is any bad behavior at all?

Mr. GOLDENBERG. Maybe. I mean, I—so yes, but I would argue— it sort of works both ways. I agree with the notion that if we had no relationship—this would basically dramatically shrink our relationship with Qatar, and then reduce our leverage over them. It would also reduce their leverage over us, so there is a bit of two sides to it. So it is a hard sort of hypothetical to make.

But I think the better option at this point is now that the military base is there, to not walk away from it for all those reasons. But to also clarify that we have other options, so this isn't a gun they could just hold to our head. I think that is where we need to be on this question.

Mr. CONNOLLY. Dr. Levitt.

Then my time is up. Thank you, Mr. Chairman.

Mr. LEVITT. So right now, we often look at the base as too big to fail, and we need it so badly that we don't really use it as much leverage, and we need to begin to use it at some leverage.

If we suddenly woke up tomorrow and there was no base, we would lose a lot of leverage, yes, but we would still have plenty of areas where we a relationship with Qatar.

In the best of circumstances, I certainly hope that we don't move the base. But I think Ilan is right, that we should start looking at what other options there might be to move some or all of it, not because we want to, but just to signal that it is not us who are over a barrel by virtue of having the base there, they are not necessarily over a barrel either, but it is a relationship. And I don't think we really use it for very much leverage right now.

Mr. SCHANZER. I would agree that we need the leverage. And what I recommend in my written testimony is that we need to do an assessment. It is not to say that we need to leave, although I think the arrangement is not sustainable. It is not, I think, the right message that we should be sending to the rest of the region. But this does not have to be binary. We can move some assets out of that base because we decide we need to redistribute, and we can't ever rely too much on the Qataris, or we might say, look, we can't move anything. But at the very least—and I think, by the way, this hearing is doing a lot of good. The Qataris know right now that we are talking about whether or not we should move the base, whether we should assess moving the base. This is incredibly important. It takes leverage away from them and puts it back in our court.

Mr. CONNOLLY. Thank you, Madam Chairman, on behalf of myself and Congresswoman Frankel.

Ms. ROS-LEHTINEN. Thank you very much. We love to hear Lois' voice, even in absentia.

And now we are so pleased to turn to Mrs. Maloney. Thank you for your patience in sitting through the subcommittee to be able ask your question.

Thank you, Carolyn, you are always welcome to be a part of our sub.

Mrs. MALONEY. Thank you, Madam Chair. And thank you for allowing me privileges to attend your committee meeting and giving me the opportunity to ask a question.

And thank you for having a hearing on a very important issue, which is a top concern to Secretary Tillerson. That is why he personally went to the region, and he has expressed his deep concern about peace and security in the region, not only for Americans and our base, but also for all of our allies.

And he publicly expressed his concern that our allies, all of the—these are all allies of America, and that he is concerned that it—if it continues, it will break up the Gulf Cooperation Council that has been an important area of cooperation with United States and our ability to collectively combat ISIS.

He also has called for the embargo, or the easing of the embargo, as it is harmful to the stability of the region, stability of the Gulf Cooperation Council, and it is difficult for our base. The embargo affects also the American base.

So his vision, I believe, is a good one, would you say, that we should figure out how to work together? We are all allies, and the enemy is not each other, but the enemy is ISIS and other terrorist activities in the region. Would you agree with Secretary Tillerson, Mr. Goldenberg?

Mr. GOLDENBERG. Yes, I would. I think that this whole crisis has been a distraction from other things we should be dealing with. You know, I am not sure I would have put as much into it has he has, necessarily, because I think that, you know, part of this is these parties have to also solve it themselves, and be responsible about that, but we can play I think a very positive role and also try to get them to de-escalate and guaranteeing any agreement and trying to push all of them in terror financing questions.

So, you know, I—I agree. For our interests, for the U.S. interests, the fact that the last 2 months in the Gulf have been spent on this instead of on all the things we prefer to be spending their time on is not good. That is the bottom line. So it would be better if we can find a way to get over this.

Sadly, I think right now, there are no indicators in the near term that is going to happen, so that we start managing the situation and also getting awful these different actors to at least tone down their public rhetoric and maximalist demands so that a few months from now, after things cool down, maybe privately they can cut some deals.

Mrs. MALONEY. Well, he has begun focusing on terrorism financing, which, I believe, is a way forward, and I understand that he has created certain criteria already for the Gulf nations to cooperate with them. And I hope that they all will. That would be a huge step forward on allowing access to their financial tracking of where money is going, if you crack down on the terrorism financing, then you are cracking down on terrorism.

Are you aware of any agreements that the State Department has made with these countries to combat terrorism financing? I was told that Qatar has entered into an agreement to share their data-base, to share their information to combat terrorism financing. Are you aware of that?

Mr. GOLDENBERG. I am, but I think, Matt, you want to——

Mr. LEVITT. Sure.

Mr. GOLDENBERG. Matt is a real expert on this.

Mr. LEVITT. So first of all, thank you for your questions.

I want to start by pointing out that there is complete consensus across this table in the need to de-escalate this crisis. And as Ilan said, we need to be focusing on the other more important issues. Several of us have also said that some of the charges already against Qatar are baseless, but some of them are very much grounded in truth, and they affect all those other issues.

Mrs. MALONEY. But my question is, are you aware of agree-ments, concrete agreements, between Qatar and the United States, or Saudi Arabia and the United States, or Bahrain, or the UAE——

Mr. LEVITT. Getting to that.

Mrs. MALONEY [continuing]. Or any of the countries specifically to work together to combat terrorism financing?

Mr. LEVITT. Yes. So that is what I was getting at. There are many agreements. There have been several of them going on for years, bilateral and otherwise. There are two new ones. One came out of the Riyadh summit, which was the agreement to set up a terror finance tracking center, the TFTC. There is no meat on those bones yet. If you look at the Treasury statements, they have lots of great ideas, I have spoken to some people who wrote those state-ments; they are aspirational. But there is great foundation there upon which we can build.

And in my previous statements, I have already pointed to that as something we can use as a face saving gesture to move forward and out of this crisis.

Mrs. MALONEY. I think that is a great idea, Dr. Levitt. We should appeal to all of these countries to join us and combat the specifics on how we would fight terrorism financing.

And I personally want to thank Secretary Tillerson for entering in with his entire effort to personally try to solve this.

We are talking about allies. We need to get together. And I am not aware of any other country that wants to host the U.S. mili-tary.

I just recall being invited to leave one country very quickly. We were told to leave Saudi Arabia, and I am not aware that any other country in the region wants to host a U.S. military.

Are you aware of any other country that wants us to come in and be there, Dr. Levitt?

Mr. LEVITT. Well, we do have bases in the UAE and Bahrain, so it is not like this is the only base we have. And I don't think the base is the ultimate issue.

If I could just add, there is one other agreement. As you noted, Secretary Tillerson signed an MOU, Memorandum of Understanding, with Qatar. This too, there is absolutely no meat on these bones, but they are very good bones, and there is more that can be built on them. I don't want people to walk away thinking, now there is an MOU, so now we can cooperate.

Mrs. MALONEY. I think that is a very important issue, Dr. Levitt. And what you could do to help us is give us exactly what kind of meat should be added to that bone, and then we should present a detailed agreement on combating terrorism financing to all of the countries in the region and see who will cooperate with us in a specific way.

I must tell you, it is deeply important to me. I represent the great city of New York, and lost 500 friends. We lost 3,000 on that day, but literally thousands and thousands more that were exposed to the deadly fumes from the terrorist attack.

So we know that there are efforts to attack New York and other cities in our—including this city. We have intelligence on that and other cities, and anything we can do with our allies to combat terrorism can save future lives in America and other places.

And I for one support Secretary Tillerson's effort to end the crisis. Let's join hands. Let's combat terrorism. Let's combat terrorism financing. Because if they can't finance their activities, they can't attack us.

I represent a district that just 6 months ago, two bombs went off. You ask where did they get the money for the bombs? How did they learn how to put them together? Who helped them? So terrorism financing is very important, I think, to the world, and especially to the United States and especially to New York City, which remains the number one terrorist target in the country.

So I want to thank all of you for your work in combating terrorism financing, and I would welcome any ideas of how we could put more strength behind efforts to combat it. And I think that if we combat it, we would also strike against the financing of terrorism activities in other countries, which allegedly, I was listening to my colleagues and their questioning, were very concerned about, and where they are teaching, you know, terrorism and we need to stop it.

My time is way, way over. I want to thank you for being here, and thank you for your work, and thank you for everything you have done to make the world safer. And thank you.

Ms. ROS-LEHTINEN. Thank you, Mrs. Maloney.

Mrs. MALONEY. Madam Chair, I don't know if I will have the chance to publicly say in your committee meeting how very, very sad you have decided to retire and leave us. You have been an incredible leader.

Ms. ROS-LEHTINEN. I am going to miss all of our colleagues.

Mrs. MALONEY. Wonderful, your leadership on this committee and as chairman of this committee has been extraordinary. First woman to head this as the chair. We are very proud of you, Ileana.

Ms. ROS-LEHTINEN. Thank you, Mrs. Maloney. Thank you so much. And feel free to come back to our subcommittee. You are a valuable member. We will make you an ex officio member. Thank you.

I have just one last wrap-up question. I know you gentlemen have been testifying for hours now.

But, Dr. Schanzer, this tension has been going on for such a long time. Why do you think that its neighbors decided to take action only now? Is there something else that you believe precipitated this?

Mr. SCHANZER. Madam Chair, thank you for the question. It is— it is really one of the questions that I think we all should have been asking all along. I think when you talk to most analysts in this town, they tell you, Well, they hate each other, it was the Brotherhood, it was the Arab Spring. Well, what made this thing erupt in the spring? There were some reports that it was, perhaps, because the Qataris paid ransom and money went to Shiite militias as well as to bad actors in Syria. But there has also been reports surfaced recently and there is a little bit of confusion over this. But I think it is worth unpacking.

There is a report from the UAE Ambassador to Russia, he went on BBC and claimed the Qataris provided intelligence about Emirati and Saudi troop movements in Yemen, and that this led directly to the death of dozens of Gulf soldiers in the Yemeni operation. I have also heard from three different sources since then that it may not have been al-Qaeda that they shared this information with but rather the Houthis and the Saleh forces in Yemen. This would be devastating for Qatar if this were to be true, because, of course, it would mean they were sharing information with Iranian proxies, which is an absolute red line for the Gulf States. So this allegedly happened in the spring. I have not been able to confirm it with a U.S. official. All I can tell you is this is what I have been hearing from people who generally know in this town.

Ms. ROS-LEHTINEN. Well, thank you very much.

And I thank the audience and the witnesses for their patience, excellent testimony. You will forgive me that I was gone a little bit from the podium. We had our bill up on the floor calling upon Iran to release the hostages, the American hostages, who are citizens and residents, and we were overwhelmingly approved. So that is why I was absent.

And with that, our subcommittee is adjourned. Thank you to all.

[Whereupon, at 4:38p.m., the subcommittee was adjourned.]

APPENDIX

MATERIAL SUBMITTED FOR THE RECORD

SUBCOMMITTEE HEARING NOTICE
COMMITTEE ON FOREIGN AFFAIRS
U.S. HOUSE OF REPRESENTATIVES
WASHINGTON, DC 20515-6128

Subcommittee on the Middle East and North Africa
Ileana Ros-Lehtinen (R-FL), Chairman

July 21, 2017

TO: MEMBERS OF THE COMMITTEE ON FOREIGN AFFAIRS

You are respectfully requested to attend an OPEN hearing of the Committee on Foreign Affairs, to be held by the Subcommittee on the Middle East and North Africa in Room 2172 of the Rayburn House Office Building (and available live on the Committee website at http://www.ForeignAffairs.house.gov):

DATE: Wednesday, July 26, 2017

TIME: 2:00 p.m.

SUBJECT: Assessing the U.S.-Qatar Relationship

WITNESSES: Jonathan Schanzer, Ph.D.
Senior Vice President
Foundation for Defense of Democracies

Matthew Levitt, Ph.D.
Director and Fromer-Wexler Fellow
Stein Program on Counterterrorism and Intelligence
The Washington Institute for Near East Policy

Mr. Ilan Goldenberg
Senior Fellow and Director
Middle East Security Program
Center for a New American Security

By Direction of the Chairman

COMMITTEE ON FOREIGN AFFAIRS

MINUTES OF SUBCOMMITTEE ON _______ *the Middle East and North Africa* _______ HEARING

Day **_Wednesday_** Date **_07/26/17_** Room **_2172_**

Starting Time **_2:16 p.m._** Ending Time **_4:38 p.m._**

Recesses [____] (____ to ____)(____ to ____)(____ to ____)(____ to ____)(____ to ____)(____ to ____)

Presiding Member(s)

Chairman Ros-Lehtinen, Rep. Wagner

Check all of the following that apply:

Open Session ☑
Executive (closed) Session ☐
Televised ☑

Electronically Recorded (taped) ☑
Stenographic Record ☑

TITLE OF HEARING:

Assessing the U.S.-Qatar Relationship

SUBCOMMITTEE MEMBERS PRESENT:

GOP- Chairman Ros-Lehtinen, Reps. Issa, Cook, DeSantis, Zeldin, Wagner, Mast, Fitzpatrick
Dem- Ranking Member Deutch, Reps. Connolly, Cicilline, Frankel, Gabbard, Schneider, Suozzi, Lieu

NON-SUBCOMMITTEE MEMBERS PRESENT: *(Mark with an * if they are not members of full committee.)*

GOP- Rep. Rohrabacher
Dem- Reps. Meeks, Jackson Lee, Maloney**

HEARING WITNESSES: Same as meeting notice attached? Yes ☑ No ☐
(If "no", please list below and include title, agency, department, or organization.)

STATEMENTS FOR THE RECORD: *(List any statements submitted for the record.)*

Statement by Mr. Connolly

TIME SCHEDULED TO RECONVENE __________
or
TIME ADJOURNED **_4:38 p.m._**

Subcommittee Staff Associate

Statement for the Record
Submitted by Mr. Connolly of Virginia

Since the opening of the U.S. Embassy in Doha in 1973, bilateral relations between the United States and Qatar have grown to encompass significant security, economic, and diplomatic dimensions. While Washington and Doha cooperate closely on many issues such as counterterrorism, the relationship is not without tension. The recent diplomatic dispute between some Gulf Cooperation Council (GCC) members and Qatar has highlighted some of these concerns, particularly regarding Qatar's financial support for terrorist groups. Nonetheless, it is not in the United States' interest for this dispute to escalate and risk broader regional instability.

Following close defense cooperation between the United States and GCC during Operation Desert Storm, Washington and Doha signed a formal Defense Cooperation Agreement (DCA) on June 23, 1992. In December 2013, the two countries renewed the DCA for another ten years. Approximately 10,000 U.S. forces are currently deployed in Qatar, most of which are based at Al Udeid air base, working as part of the Coalition Forward Air Component Command (CFACC). The air field also hosts the forward headquarters for U.S. Central Command (CENTCOM). The U.S. military's strategic facilities in Qatar were key to Operation Iraqi Freedom and remain critical to Operation Inherent Resolve, which is combatting the Islamic State in Iraq and Syria. Qatar has been a large consumer of U.S. foreign military sales, including a purchase in November 2016 of up to 72 F-15QA aircraft worth more than $21 billion.

Despite close U.S.-Qatari security relations, on June 5, 2017, Saudi Arabia, the United Arab Emirates, Bahrain, and Egypt cut off diplomatic and economic relations with Qatar, citing Doha's close ties with Iran and support for terrorism. The GCC states assert that Qatar continues to support Islamist extremist groups in the region, including al-Qaeda, Hamas, the Taliban, and the Muslim Brotherhood, in violation of a series of secret agreements with its Gulf neighbors. The United States has also designated several of these groups as foreign terrorist organizations, and has pressured Doha to punish individual terrorist financiers and pursue systemic solutions to terror financing originating within its borders.

This month, Secretary of State Rex Tillerson traveled to the region to attempt to negotiate a resolution to the crisis. Rather than helping to broker a solution to this dispute among our GCC partners, President Trump has only exacerbated the situation by choosing sides. Trump has stoked regional rivalries and inflamed conflict in an already volatile part of the world. Criticism of Qatar is valid. They should be doing more to combat terrorism. However, uninformed missives that do not take into account the location and well-being of 10,000 U.S. service members are reckless and disturbing. I look forward to hearing from our witnesses regarding how the United States can play a moderating role in the ongoing Qatar-GCC dispute and seize opportunities to promote U.S. interests in our relationship with Qatar.